LERNKRIMI ENGLISCH

Sprachkurs Englisch
für Anfänger

Alison Romer und Gesa Füßle

compact

Weitere Informationen zu Compact Lernkrimis finden Sie am Ende des Buches und unter www.lernkrimi.de.

Baierbrunner Straße 27, 81379 München
Ausgabe 2013
3. Auflage

Chefredaktion: Dr. Matthias Feldbaum
Redaktion: Helga Aichele
Produktion: Frank Speicher
Illustrationen: Karl Knospe
Lernkrimi-Logo: Carsten Abelbeck
Gestaltung: textum GmbH
Umschlaggestaltung: Hartmut Baier
Sprecher: Martin Brown, Andreas Füßle, Azhar Kemal, Sophie Lloyd, Liz Smith

ISBN: 978-3-8174-7784-5
7277842/3

www.compactverlag.de, www.lernkrimi.de

Spannend Englisch lernen mit dem bekannten Lernkrimi-Inspector James Hudson. Erleben Sie ihn in seinem Alltag und auf Verbrecherjagd – und helfen Sie ihm, den Fall zu lösen. Im Gegenzug wird er Sie mit zahlreichen Tipps zum Sprachenlernen belohnen.
Die Lektionen sind nach der 30-Minuten-Methode aufgebaut: Für jede Doppelseite sollten Sie in etwa 30 Minuten benötigen. Seien Sie jedoch nicht beunruhigt, wenn Sie einmal länger brauchen. In jedem Fall gilt: Teilen Sie sich das Lernen ein! Wenn Sie täglich eine halbe Stunde Englisch lernen, werden Sie schon bald Erfolge sehen. Und Sie werden sich das Gelernte durch tägliches Training besser merken können, als wenn Sie nur selten und dafür länger Englisch lernen. Am Ende des Sprachkurses können Sie so das Niveau A2 des gemeinsamen europäischen Referenzrahmens erreichen.

Jede Doppelseite bildet eine in sich abgeschlossene Unterlektion, in der Sie nicht nach einer bestimmten Reihenfolge vorgehen müssen. Obwohl der Grammatikteil erst am Ende der Doppelseite steht, können Sie ihn sich natürlich auch als erstes durchlesen. Empfehlenswert ist jedoch, sich möglichst viel selbst aus dem Kontext zu erschließen, da es sich auf diese Weise leichter einprägt.

Alle Texte und Dialoge sind auf CD vertont und helfen Ihnen so beim Hör- und Leseverstehen. Zusätzlich trainieren viele ebenfalls vertonte Übungen gezielt die Aussprache.

Die Grammatikzusammenfassungen an jedem Lektionsende und die drei Wiederholungslektionen helfen Ihnen, das Gelernte zu vertiefen. Im Abschlusstest können Sie Ihren Erfolg konkret messen.

In jeder Lektion finden Sie sogenannte Rätselkärtchen mit Fragen, die pro Lektion ein Lösungswort ergeben. Auf www.lernkrimi.de/download-vokabelkarten/ können Sie mit diesem Lösungswort als Passwort Vokabelkarten für die entsprechende Lektion herunterladen und ausdrucken. So haben Sie auch unterwegs den Sprachkurs immer dabei! Doch auch, wenn Sie von dem Angebot keinen Gebrauch machen möchten, empfehlen wir Ihnen, die Lösungswörter zu finden, denn sie helfen Ihnen, den Bösewicht zu entlarven.

Viel Spaß und Erfolg beim Englischlernen!

INHALT

1.1 SMALL TALK

1-1

My name is James Hudson. I am a policeman. I eat toast with butter and a boiled egg. I drink tea. I read The Times newspaper. “Look at this,” I say to Miss Paddington. She comes into the kitchen. “The newspaper reports a burglary in a jewellery shop.”

“Oh, stop reading that, Inspector,” she says. “Here is your mail!”

I take the letters and open them. Two letters are bills: one for the electricity and one for the phone. I open the last letter. It is from my boss.

To: Inspector Hudson
Invitation to a party
at 263 Bacon Street, London
on Saturday at 8.00 p.m.
Bring a friend
From: Sir Reginald of Scotland Yard

1-2

ÜBUNG 1:

Hören Sie sich die englischen Sätze an und sprechen Sie nach! Verbinden Sie die Sätze mit ihrer Übersetzung!

1. ☐ I eat toast with butter.	a) Hier ist Ihre Post.
2. ☐ I read the newspaper.	b) Ich trinke Tee.
3. ☐ The newspaper reports a burglary.	c) Zwei Briefe sind Rechnungen.
4. ☐ I drink tea.	d) Ich esse Toast mit Butter.
5. ☐ Here is your mail.	e) Die Zeitung berichtet von einem Einbruch.
6. ☐ Two letters are bills.	f) Ich lese Zeitung.

ÜBUNG 2:

My name is James Hudson. I am a policeman. I work for Scotland Yard.
Miss Paddington works for Inspector Hudson. She is a housekeeper.

Schreiben Sie über sich selbst!

1. My name is ______________________________
2. I work for ______________________________
3. My address is ______________________________

KRIMIVOKABULAR

police – Polizei
policeman – Polizist(in)
burglary – Einbruch
burglar – Einbrecher(in)
to burgle – einbrechen

ÜBUNG 3:

Hören und lesen Sie gleichzeitig die folgenden Wochentage! Sprechen Sie nach!

1-3

1. Saturday
2. Friday
3. Wednesday
4. Sunday
5. Thursday
6. Tuesday
7. Monday

Rätselkärtchen

Richtig ✓ oder falsch ×?	✓	×
Sunday = Sonntag	p	r
Hudson = housekeeper	i	o

ÜBUNG 4:

Bringen Sie die oben genannten Wochentage in die richtige Reihenfolge! Versuchen Sie, sich an Ähnlichkeiten zu orientieren!

1. Montag: ____________________
2. Dienstag: ____________________
3. Mittwoch: ____________________
4. Donnerstag: ____________________
5. Freitag: ____________________
6. Samstag: ____________________
7. Sonntag: ____________________

GRAMMATIK

Das Verb *to say* (sagen)

I say	ich sage	*we say*	wir sagen
you say	du sagst/Sie sagen	*you say*	ihr sagt/Sie sagen
he/she/it says	er/sie/es sagt	*they say*	sie sagen

! ***You*** kann sowohl **du** als auch **ihr** oder **Sie** bedeuten. Es wird also kein Unterschied gemacht, ob man jemanden siezt oder duzt – oder ob man mit einer oder mehreren Personen spricht!

Das Verb *to be* (sein)

! Wie das deutsche **sein** ist das englische ***to be*** unregelmäßig.

Im **Simple Present** (Gegenwart) lauten die Verbformen von ***to be*** wie folgt:

I am	ich bin	*we are*	wir sind
you are	du bist/Sie sind	*you are*	ihr seid/Sie sind
he/she/it is	er/sie/es ist	*they are*	sie sind

! ***I*** **(ich)** wird immer groß geschrieben!

1.2 SMALL TALK

1-4

At 8.00 p.m. my taxi stops at Sir Reginald's house on Bacon Street. I get out. Miss Paddington gets out too. "I'm so happy to be here!" she says.
Tonight she wears a long black dress. She looks like an opera singer.
"Elvira is here, too," I say.
The house is very big. Sir Reginald comes to the door. "Hudson!" he says. "I'm very happy to see you."
We shake hands. I can hear piano music.
"And Miss Paddington!" says Sir Reginald. "You look lovely tonight, Miss P. Come in, come in."
We go into the living room. There are many people, and everybody has a glass of champagne.
A man plays the piano.
"It's wonderful!" says Miss Paddington.

ÜBUNG 1:

Setzen Sie die folgenden Begriffe ein! ***(are, have, is (2x), read)***

1. My name __________ Inspector Hudson.
2. You __________ my friend.
3. She __________ very happy.
4. Every morning I __________ breakfast.
5. I __________ The Times newspaper.

Rätselkärtchen

A man __________ the piano. f
drinks l
plays

My __________ is Hudson. e
dress i
name

ÜBUNG 2:

Übersetzen Sie!

1. I eat ____________________
2. they drink ____________________
3. he can ____________________
4. she gets out ____________________
5. we hear ____________________
6. you play ____________________
7. to wear ____________________
8. big ____________________

9. wonderful ____________________ 11. dress ____________________

10. happy ____________________ 12. black ____________________

Inspector Hudson empfiehlt:

Hören Sie sich den Text zunächst an, ohne ins Buch zu schauen. Lesen Sie erst mit, wenn Sie ihn das zweite Mal anhören. So bekommen Sie ein besseres Gefühl für die Sprache.

ÜBUNG 3:

Hören Sie zu und setzen Sie die fehlenden Begriffe ein! Sprechen Sie die Sätze nach!
(work, to be, I'm, dress, big, name)

1-5

My (1.) ____________ is Miss Paddington. I (2.) ____________ for Inspector Hudson. (3.) ____________ a housekeeper. Sir Reginald's house is very (4.) ____________. I'm very happy (5.) ______ ______ here. I wear my long black (6.) ____________ when I go to parties.

GRAMMATIK

Jeder, jede, jedes ...

Every *morning I drink tea.* — **Jeden** Morgen trinke ich Tee.
Everybody *has a glass of champagne.* — **Jeder** hat/trinkt ein Glas Sekt.

Das Verb im Präsens

Bei Verben in der 3. Person Singular (*he/she/it*) fügen wir ein **s** hinzu, z. B:
*he/she/it work****s*** — *he/she/it eat****s***

to have (haben)

I have	ich habe	*we have*	wir haben
you have	du hast	*you have*	ihr habt/Sie haben
he/she/it has	er/sie/es hat	*they have*	sie haben

Kurzformen

In der gesprochenen Sprache und in persönlichen E-Mails verwenden wir Kurzformen:

I'm = I am	*he's = he is*	*we're = we are*
you're = you are	*she's = she is*	*they're = they are*

1.3 SMALL TALK

1-6

Elvira is next to the piano. A man stands next to her. They talk.
"I think he's a professor," says Miss Paddington. "He's very clever."
Sir Reginald gives a glass of champagne to me and a glass to Miss Paddington. His champagne is very good.
"Do you like caviar, Miss P?" he asks. "My caviar is delicious. Come with me."
They go into the dining room.
I smile and wave at Elvira. Her hair is red and her dress is green. She looks really lovely. Elvira is an insurance investigator. Sometimes we work together. She likes to help solve crime. I say hello.

ÜBUNG 1:

1-7

Hören Sie zu und setzen Sie die fehlenden Begriffe ein! Sprechen Sie die Sätze nach!
(how are, nice, this is (2x), fine)

Elvira: Hello Inspector. How are you?

Inspector Hudson: (1.) __________, thanks. And you? (2.) ________________ you?

Elvira: I'm fine. (3.) ________________ my friend, Victor Crawley.

Inspector Hudson: Nice to meet you.

Elvira: Victor, (4.) ____________ Inspector Hudson.

Victor: (5.) _____________ to meet you too, Inspector.

Rätselkärtchen

Richtig ✓ oder falsch ×?

	✓	×
Elvira = red hair	c	p
Sir Reginald = professor	m	e

ÜBUNG 2:

Setzen Sie die korrekten Kurzformen ein!

1. *It's* my house. (it)
2. ______ my date. (he)
3. ______ his housekeeper. (she)
4. ______ her friend. (I)
5. ______ your party. (it)

ÜBUNG 3:

Bringen Sie die nachfolgenden Sätze in die richtige Reihenfolge, so dass das Gespräch einen Sinn ergibt!

1. Nice to meet you, Victor.
2. Fine, thanks. And you?
3. Hello. How are you?
4. Nice to meet you too, Inspector.
5. I'm good, thanks.
6. This is my friend Victor.
7. And Victor, this is the Inspector.

Lösung: __ __ __ __ __ __ __

KRIMIVOKABULAR

to solve – lösen, aufklären
crime – Verbrechen
criminal – Verbrecher(in)
investigation – Ermittlung
to investigate – ermitteln

ÜBUNG 4:

Bilden Sie die Kurzformen!

1. we are: ________	3. he is: ________	5. they are: ________	7. I am: ________
2. it is: ________	4. you are: ________	6. she is: ________	8. here is: ________

ÜBUNG 5:

Hören Sie sich das Alphabet an und sprechen Sie nach!

1-8

A B C D E F G H I J K L M N O P Q R S T U V W X Y Z

GRAMMATIK

Das Possessivpronomen

Possessivpronomen drücken den Besitz oder die Zugehörigkeit aus:

my *date* (**meine** Verabredung)
his *house* (**sein** Haus)

I	***my***	*she*	***her***
you	***your***	*it*	***its***
he	***his***	*we*	***our***
		they	***their***

ÜBUNG 6:

Buchstabieren Sie die folgenden Wörter laut. Hören Sie anschließend die CD und überprüfen Sie die Antworten!

1-9

1. Hudson
2. extra
3. Elvira
4. piano
5. insurance
6. alphabet

1-10

"I often read about you in the newspapers," says Victor. "You are famous, Inspector!"
"And you? What do you do?" I ask.
"I'm a professor of Criminology at the university," he answers.
"That's interesting," I say. "Do you like to solve crimes?"
Victor smiles.
"No, I like to study them," he says. "I like to study crimes that can't be solved."
Elvira laughs.
"All crimes can be solved," she says. "Inspector Hudson can solve them."
"Really?" says Victor.

1-11

ÜBUNG 1:

Hören Sie zu und setzen Sie die fehlenden Begriffe ein!
(help, solve, he's, card, thanks, gets, glass)

"There's a good team at Scotland Yard," Inspector Hudson says. "We (1.) ____________ most crimes."
"That's good," says Victor Crawley.
Victor (2.) ______________ more champagne for Elvira.
"(3.) ____________ very intelligent," Hudson says. "How do you know him?"
"From my office."
Victor comes back with a (4.) ____________ of champagne. He gives it to Elvira.
"Thanks," she says.
"Here is my (5.) ____________, Inspector," Victor says. He gives Hudson a card. "Maybe I can (6.) ____________ you one day."
"(7.) ____________," says the Inspector. He takes the business card.

Rätselkärtchen

Was stimmt?

Inspector Hudson solves crimes. **m**

Inspector Hudson can't solve crimes. **s**

ÜBUNG 2:

Verbinden Sie die passenden Sätze miteinander! Hören Sie danach die Sätze auf der CD und sprechen Sie nach!

1-12

1. ☐ What do you do?
2. ☐ This is my friend Victor.
3. ☐ Here is your champagne.
4. ☐ Do you like to solve crimes?
5. ☐ How are you?
6. ☐ Can you help me?

a) Nice to meet you.
b) No, I can't.
c) Fine, thanks.
d) I'm a policeman.
e) Thanks.
f) Yes, I do.

ÜBUNG 3:

Hören Sie zu und beantworten Sie die gehörten Fragen!

1-13

1. *I'm* ______________________
2. *Yes,* ______________________
3. ______________________ *policeman.*

GRAMMATIK

How are you?
Fine, thanks. oder *I'm fine, thanks.*   *OK, thanks.* oder *I'm OK, thanks.*

Zustimmung/Verneinung
Jetzt können Sie sagen, ob Sie etwas können oder nicht:

yes = ja   **no** = nein   **not** = nicht
can = können   **can't** = nicht können
can't ist die Kurzform von **cannot.**

***Can** you read?* ***Yes**, I **can** read.*   ***Can** she help?* ***No**, she **can't** help.*

Oft werden die Antworten nur verkürzt:
***Can** you read?* ***Yes**, I **can**.*   ***Can** she help?* ***No**, she **can't**.*

Nach ***like*** folgt das Verb im Infinitiv mit ***to***. So können Sie sagen, was Sie mögen:
*I **like to** read.*   *He **likes to** solve crime.*

Sie können natürlich auch Dinge mögen:
*I **like** tea.*   *Miss Paddington **likes** champagne.*

Herzlichen Glückwunsch! Sie sind am Ende der ersten Lektion angelangt. Jetzt haben Sie die Gelegenheit, die Grammatik noch etwas intensiver zu betrachten und das Lösungswort für die Vokabelkärtchen der ersten Lektion zu knacken.

Das Verb
Im **Simple Present** (Präsens) bleibt das Verb immer unverändert, außer in der 3. Person Singular: *to wear – I wear – she wear**s***.

ÜBUNG 1:
Setzen Sie die Verben in ihrer richtigen Form in die Lücken ein!

This (1. be) ____________ Inspector Hudson. He (2. drink) ________________ tea. Miss Paddington (3. be) ____________ his housekeeper. She (4. wear) ______________ a long black dress.
"You (5. look) _______________ like an opera singer, Miss Paddington!" (6. say) _____________ Inspector Hudson. They (7. go) ________________ to a party. Sir Reginald (8. bring) ________________ champagne. Miss Paddington (9. like) _______________ champagne.

Das Personalpronomen
Im Englischen muss man kein Geschlecht zu den Substantiven lernen! Männliche Menschen und Tiere sind immer männlich, also ***he***, weibliche Menschen und weibliche Tiere sind ***she*** und alle Dinge und Tiere, deren Geschlecht man nicht kennt, sind ***it***.
Elvira talks to Victor. ***He*** *is a professor.*
I like Miss Paddington. ***She*** *is a housekeeper.*
I open the letter. ***It*** *is from my boss.*

Der Artikel
Ob der unbestimmte Artikel ***a*** oder ***an*** benutzt wird, hängt vom ersten Laut des folgenden Wortes ab: ***a*** wird benutzt, wenn der nachfolgende Laut ein Konsonant ist, ***an*** vor einem Vokal.

a s*inger* ***a b****oiled egg*
an e*gg* ***an o****pera singer*

Der bestimmte Artikel ist immer ***the***. Allerdings wird er vor einem Wort, das mit einem Vokal beginnt, mit langem ***i*** [ðiː] ausgesprochen.

ÜBUNG 2:

Setzen Sie den richtigen unbestimmten Artikel ein!

1. ________ inspector
2. ________ professor
3. ________ house
4. ________ egg
5. ________ toast

Rätselkärtchen

Sind die folgenden Sätze grammatikalisch richtig?

	✓	×
The policeman eats an eggs.	t	a
Miss Paddington drinks champagne.	n	o

Lösungswort für Lektion 1: _ _ _ _ _ _ _ _ _ _

Die Vokabelkärtchen gibt es auf **www.lernkrimi.de**

(!) Berufe werden **immer** mit dem unbestimmten Artikel angegeben:

*I'm **a** policeman.* *He's **a** professor.*

*She's **a** housekeeper.* *You're **an** inspector.*

ÜBUNG 3:

Schlagen Sie im Wörterbuch nach, wie Ihr Beruf auf Englisch heißt! Stellen Sie sich möglichst ausführlich vor! (Name, Arbeitgeber, Beruf, Wohnort)

____

____

____

____

Das Possessivpronomen

Das Possessivpronomen zeigt den Besitz oder die Zugehörigkeit an. Es passt sich in seiner Form an den „Besitzer" an (*my, your, his* usw.), jedoch in keiner Weise an das Objekt (vgl. Deutsch: mein, meine ...)

***my** boiled egg* ***my** housekeeper* ***my** inspector*

ÜBUNG 4:

Setzen Sie das passende Possessivpronomen ein!

1. They drink ____________ tea.
2. You read ____________ newspaper.
3. We help ____________ policeman.
4. He eats ____________ egg.
5. She opens ____________ letter.
6. I meet ____________ boss.

1-14

The next morning I call Elvira.
"How are you?" I ask.
"Good, thanks," she says. "It was a wonderful party."
"You have an interesting friend," I say.
"Yes, Victor is very intelligent," she replies.
"Shall we meet for coffee?" I ask.

1-15

ÜBUNG 1:

Hören Sie zu und setzen Sie die fehlenden Begriffe ein!
(later, nice, when, breakfast, afternoon)

Elvira: Yes, great! (1.) ____________ shall we meet?

Inspector Hudson: Is this (2.) ________________ okay?

Elvira: Yes, this afternoon is good. There's a (3.) ________________ café on Castle Street. But I have to go now. Victor and I are having a lovely (4.) ______________.

Inspector Hudson: No problem. See you (5.) ______________.

Elvira: Bye, James.

ÜBUNG 2:

Beantworten Sie die Fragen auf Deutsch!

1. Wen ruft James Hudson an? ______________________________
2. Was macht Elvira gerade? ______________________________
3. Wo verabreden sich Hudson und Elvira? ______________________________

1-16

ÜBUNG 3:

Hören Sie sich die Aussprache der folgenden Wörter an und sprechen Sie nach! Verbinden Sie die Wörter mit ihrer Übersetzung!

1. ☐ wonderful	2. ☐ interesting	3. ☐ intelligent	4. ☐ nice	5. ☐ lovely
a) intelligent	b) nett	c) schön	d) wunderbar	e) interessant

ÜBUNG 4:

Setzen Sie in die Lücken die passenden Fragewörter ein! ***(when, where, what)***

1. __________ shall we meet? – On Saturday.
2. __________ shall we meet? – At the café.
3. __________ do you drink? – Coffee.

Rätselkärtchen

Richtig ✓ oder falsch ×?

	✓	×
interesting = interessant	i	e
morning = Morgen	n	v

ÜBUNG 5:

Bringen Sie die nachfolgenden Sätze in die richtige Reihenfolge, so dass das Gespräch einen Sinn ergibt!

1. Great! When shall we meet?
2. See you later.
3. 4.00 is fine. See you later.
4. I'm fine, thanks. Would you like to meet for a coffee?
5. Good, thanks. And you?
6. Let's meet at 4.00.
7. Hi, how are you?

Lösung:

__ __ __ __ __ __ __

GRAMMATIK

Das Fragewort

Beginnen Sie offene Fragen, die nicht einfach mit **ja** oder **nein** beantwortet werden können, mit folgenden Fragewörtern:

what?	was?	***why?***	warum?
when?	wann?	***which?***	welche/r/s?
how?	wie?		

!

who?	wer?
where?	wo?

Das Adjektiv

Adjektive vermitteln Informationen über Menschen oder Dinge. Sie sind also beschreibende Wörter.

She's an ***intelligent*** *woman.* *It's a* ***nice*** *day.* *The party is* ***wonderful****.*

Das Verb ***shall*** (sollen)

Shall wird in Fragen meistens dann benutzt, wenn man ein Angebot oder einen Vorschlag macht oder wenn man die Meinung eines anderen erfahren möchte.

What ***shall*** *we eat?*	Was **wollen** wir essen?
Shall *I open the window?*	**Soll** ich das Fenster öffnen?
Shall *we go to the cinema tonight?*	**Sollen** wir heute Abend ins Kino gehen?

2.2 TELEPHONE

1-17

I go to my office at Scotland Yard. It's Sunday. It's very quiet. Most people are at home. The rooms are empty. I start to work. Suddenly the telephone rings. I answer it.
"Hello," I say. "Hudson speaking."
There is no reply.
"Hello," I say again. "Who is that?"
Silence.
I hang up.
"Strange," I think.
Then there is a knock on my door.
"Come in!" I say.
Sir Reginald opens the door.
"Hello Hudson," he says. "Why are you here today?"
"I'm here to work," I say. "It's nice and quiet."
Suddenly the phone rings again.
"Hello, Hudson speaking," I say.
Silence. "Hello!" I say again.

1-18

ÜBUNG 1:

Fügen Sie die Übersetzung der angegebenen Wörter ein! Hören Sie danach den Text auf der CD!

A deep voice (1. sagt) _______________ something.

Inspector Hudson (2. fragt) _______________ the person (3. wer) _______________ he is.

The caller does not (4. antworten) _______________. Then (5. er) _______________ says that Inspector Hudson is in danger. Hudson (6. ist) _______________ frightened. The (7. Anrufer) _______________ hangs up.

Hudson (8. denkt) _______________ somebody wants to murder him.

1-19

ÜBUNG 2:

***This** or **that**? **These** or **those**? Hören Sie zu und setzen Sie das korrekte Wort ein!*

The phone rings.
"Hello," says Hudson.

"Hello, is (1.) ____________ Inspector Hudson?" asks Ann.
"Yes, (2.) ____________ is Hudson. Who is calling, please?" Hudson says.
"(3.) ____________ is Constable Ann Watson."
"Hi, Constable. How can I help you?"
"Can we meet to talk about (4.) ____________ strange phone calls?" Ann asks.
"Of course," says Hudson. "(5.) ____________ calls are frightening. Please come to my office."

Rätselkärtchen

Hudson ____________ the phone.
[t] thinks [s] answers

Most people ____________ at home.
[p] are [a] is

ÜBUNG 3:

Markieren Sie die höflichere Variante!

1. ☐ a) Who is calling, please? ☐ b) Who is it?
2. ☐ a) What do you want? ☐ b) How can I help you?
3. ☐ a) Of course. ☐ b) Yes.
4. ☐ a) Please come to my office. ☐ b) Come to my office.
5. ☐ a) Do you want coffee? ☐ b) Would you like a coffee?

GRAMMATIK

James Hudson speaking. **Nicht:** *Hudson is speaking.*
Hello, Hudson here. **Nicht:** *Here is Hudson.*

Höflichkeit

Im Englischen ist es besonders wichtig, sich höflich auszudrücken.

This oder *that?*

Mehr als im Deutschen wird im Englischen zwischen ***this*** (diese/r/s hier) und ***that*** (jene/r/s dort) unterschieden. In Übung 2 sehen Sie die Verwendung. Die Pluralformen sind ***these*** (diese hier) und ***those*** (jene dort).
This *is my book,* ***that*** *is your book.*
These *are nice flowers,* ***those*** *are not nice.*

No

No heißt nicht nur **nein**, sondern auch **kein**.

No *problem.* **Kein** Problem.
I have ***no*** *money.* Ich habe **kein** Geld.
No *reply.* **Keine** Antwort.

2.3 TELEPHONE

1-20

Constable Ann Watson sits next to me.

"Now, Inspector Hudson," she says, "tell me about the calls."

"There were two calls. Both were around 11 o'clock," I answer.

The constable writes my answer in her notebook.

"Who was the caller?" she asks.

"I don't know."

"Was it a man or a woman?"

"A man," I say. "A man with a deep voice."

"What did he say?" she asks.

"'You are in danger'," I reply. "But I think it's a joke, Constable Watson. Don't you think so?"

"Maybe. Maybe not," she says. "We will install a phone tap at your office and your home. We will find this man."

ÜBUNG 1:

Welches sind die vier Fragen in dem obigen Text? Schreiben Sie sie auf!

1. ______________________________
2. ______________________________
3. ______________________________
4. ______________________________

ÜBUNG 2:

Lesen Sie den obigen Text nochmals durch und finden Sie die Vergangenheitsformen ***(Simple Past)*** *der folgenden Wörter!*

1. do ____________ 3. are ____________

2. is ____________

Inspector Hudson empfiehlt:

Zählen Sie! Zählen Sie alles, was Ihnen begegnet, die Stifte auf Ihrem Schreibtisch, die Lampen in Ihrem Zimmer ... So bekommen Sie schnell ein Gefühl für die Zahlen.

ÜBUNG 3:

Hören Sie sich die Zahlen an und sprechen Sie nach!

1-21

1 one	6 six	11 eleven	16 sixteen
2 two	7 seven	12 twelve	17 seventeen
3 three	8 eight	13 thirteen	18 eighteen
4 four	9 nine	14 fourteen	19 nineteen
5 five	10 ten	15 fifteen	20 twenty

ÜBUNG 4:

Schreiben Sie die Uhrzeiten auf! Hören Sie danach die Sätze auf der CD und sprechen Sie nach!

1-22

1.  It's ______________ o'clock.
2.  It's ______________ o'clock.
3.  It's ______________ o'clock.
4.  It's ______________ o'clock.
5.  It's ______________ o'clock.

GRAMMATIK

Das Simple Past

Wenn man nach etwas fragt, das in der Vergangenheit stattfand, benutzt man das **Simple Past**.

Simple Present	**Simple Past**
*Who **is** it?*	*Who **was** it?*
*Where **are** they?*	*Where **were** they?*

Die Uhrzeit

Im Englischen geht man nicht nach der 24-Stunden-Uhr, sondern verwendet die Zahlen von eins bis zwölf zusammen mit ***a.m.*** (vor zwölf Uhr mittags) und ***p.m.*** (nach zwölf Uhr mittags):

8:00 Uhr *8.00 a.m.* 20:00 Uhr *8.00 p.m.*

Wenn ohnehin klar ist, um welche Tageszeit es sich handelt, kann man die Angabe ***a.m./p.m.*** weglassen.

TELEPHONE

1-23

The constable goes back to her office.
I put on my coat. It is time to meet Elvira.
Suddenly the phone rings again. I'm shocked. I answer it.
"Hello?" I say.
"Inspector Hudson?"
It's Miss Paddington.
"Hello? Are you there?" she asks.
"Yes, I'm here."
"Sir Reginald says you're in danger!"
"No, I'm not."
"Come home!" says Miss Paddington. "You're not safe."
"I'm very safe," I reply. "I'm at Scotland Yard. Criminals can't come in here. Now, I'm late for coffee with Elvira. Goodbye, Miss Paddington. Don't worry."
"But Inspector …" Miss Paddington starts to say.
"Goodbye," I say. I hang up.

KRIMIVOKABULAR

safe – Safe
safe – sicher
danger – Gefahr
dangerous – gefährlich

1-24

ÜBUNG 1:

Hören Sie sich die englischen Sätze an und sprechen Sie nach! Übersetzen Sie!

1. Are you there? ______________________
2. You are in danger. ______________________
3. No, I'm not. ______________________
4. Come home. ______________________
5. I'm late. ______________________
6. Don't worry. ______________________

1-25

ÜBUNG 2:

Bilden Sie Fragen mit den Fragewörtern in Klammern! Hören Sie danach die Fragen auf der CD und sprechen Sie nach!

1. are you going? *Where are you going?* (where)
2. is calling? ______________________ (who)

3. do you do? ______________________ (what)

4. shall we meet? ______________________ (when)

5. is he in danger? ______________________ (why)

6. are you? ______________________ (how)

Rätselkärtchen

Was stimmt?

Miss Paddington is not safe. g

Miss Paddington rings Inspector Hudson. t

ÜBUNG 3:

*Markieren Sie den Satz im **Past Tense**!*

1. ☐ a) What do you do? ☐ b) What did you do?
2. ☐ a) Who was that? ☐ b) Who is that?
3. ☐ a) Was it a man or a woman? ☐ b) Is it a man or a woman?
4. ☐ a) Where did you go? ☐ b) Where are you going?

ÜBUNG 4:

Übersetzen Sie ins Englische!

1. Komm nach Hause! ______________________
2. Gehen Sie zu Scotland Yard! ______________________
3. Macht euch keine Sorgen! ______________________
4. Sei vorsichtig! ______________________

GRAMMATIK

Der Imperativ

Man benutzt den Imperativ für Befehle und Aufforderungen. Er wird einfach mit dem Infinitiv (der Grundform) des Verbs gebildet:

***Come** home!*	**Komm/kommt/kommen Sie** nach Hause!
***Be** careful!*	**Sei/seid/seien Sie** vorsichtig!

Soll etwas **nicht** getan werden, wird das Verb mit ***don't (do not)*** verneint.

***Don't** worry!*	Mach dir/macht euch/machen Sie sich keine Sorgen!

Die Frage

Die Fragewörter kennen Sie bereits. Beachten Sie jedoch, dass sie nicht immer genau wie im Deutschen verwendet werden:

***What** is your name?*	**Wie** heißt du/heißen Sie?
***What** time is it?*	**Wie** spät ist es?

Where kann auch benutzt werden, um nach der Richtung zu fragen:

***Where** do you go?*	**Wohin** gehst du/gehen Sie?

Fragen ohne Fragewort werden fast ausschließlich mit ***to do*** formuliert:

***Do** you like caviar?*	**Mögen** Sie Kaviar?

ÜBUNG 1:

Setzen Sie das richtige Fragewort ein!

1. Hello. ________________ are you?
2. I don't know her. ______________ is she?
3. ________________ do you live?
4. ________________ is your name?
5. ________________ does Inspector Hudson work? – At Scotland Yard.

Rätselkärtchen

Sind die folgenden Sätze grammatikalisch richtig?

	✓	×
How is your name?	u	o
I'm fine, thanks.	r	k

Lösungswort für Lektion 2: _ _ _ _ _ _ _ _ _

Die Vokabelkärtchen gibt es auf **www.lernkrimi.de**

Das Adjektiv

Im Englischen sind die Adjektive unveränderlich. Anders als im Deutschen passen sie sich also nie dem Substantiv an:

*A **tall** man.*	Ein groß**er** Mann.	*The man is **tall**.*	Der Mann ist groß.
*A **fat** woman.*	Eine dick**e** Frau.	*The woman is **fat**.*	Die Frau ist dick.
*An **old** house.*	Ein alt**es** Haus.	*The house is **old**.*	Das Haus ist alt.
*Those **lovely** flowers.*		Jene schön**en** Blumen.	
*Those flowers are **lovely**.*		Jene Blumen sind schön.	

ÜBUNG 2:

Unterstreichen Sie die Adjektive!

Inspector Hudson is a good policeman. Miss Paddington works for him. She makes him a lovely breakfast with hot tea. It's Sunday. It's nice and quiet. There are no strange phone calls. Elvira Elliot has red hair and a red car. Victor has nice hair. The party yesterday was wonderful.

No

Wie Sie bereits wissen, kann ***no*** außer **nein** auch **kein** bedeuten. In dem Fall wird es an die Stelle des Artikels gesetzt:

– *Do you have **a** car?*	– Hast du/haben Sie **ein** Auto?
– *No, I have **no** car.*	– Nein, ich habe **kein** Auto.

(!) ***No*** und ***to know*** (wissen) werden gleich ausgesprochen!

ÜBUNG 3:

Beantworten Sie die Fragen verneinend!

1. Does Miss Paddington have a housekeeper? *No, she has no housekeeper.*
2. Is there a reply when Hudson answers the phone?

   ____

3. Was there a strange phone call?

   ____

4. Do you have a book?

   ____

Die Frage mit *to do* im Simple Past

Bisher haben Sie die Vergangenheitsform des Verbs ***to be*** kennengelernt: ***was/were***.

Bei Fragen, die mit ***to do*** gebildet werden, wird nur das Hilfsverb **do** in die Vergangenheit gesetzt:

*Where **do** you **go**?*	*Where **did** you **go**?*
*What **do** you **do**?*	*What **did** you **do**?*
*What **does** he **say**?*	*What **did** he **say**?*

KRIMIVOKABULAR

to murder – umbringen
murder – Mord
murderer – Mörder(in)

ÜBUNG 4:

*Setzen Sie **Simple Present** ins **Simple Past** und umgekehrt!*

1. Victor is intelligent.	*Victor was intelligent.*
2. Who is the caller?	______________________________
3. ______________________________	Was it a man or a woman?
4. There are two letters.	______________________________
5. What do you write?	______________________________

3.1 AT THE CAFÉ

1-26

It's a quarter to four. Elvira is sitting in the café. She is drinking a cup of coffee. She is waiting for me.
"Sorry, I'm late," I say. I sit down next to her.
"No problem," she says.
The café is full of people. Everyone is talking and laughing. They're drinking coffee and eating cake.
"Would you like tea or coffee?" Elvira asks.
"I'd like a cup of tea," I say.
"Do you take milk?"
"No, thanks."
"Do you take sugar?"
"Yes, two sugars, please."

1-27

ÜBUNG 1:

Hören Sie sich das Gespräch zwischen Elvira und dem Kellner an und setzen Sie die fehlenden Begriffe ein!
(with, please, I'd like, anything, what, how)

Waiter: Hello. (1.) ____________ can I get you?
Elvira: (2.) ______________ a cup of coffee, please.
Waiter: Black, or (3.) _____________ milk?
Elvira: Just black, thanks.
Waiter: (4.) ______________ else?
Elvira: No, thanks. (5.) ______________ much is that?
Waiter: That's one pound fifty, (6.) _______________.
Elvira: Thanks.

Rätselkärtchen

Richtig ✓ oder falsch ×?

	✓	×
Elvira drinks coffee.	c	s
Hudson takes sugar.	h	t

1-28

ÜBUNG 2:

*Bilden Sie Sätze im **Present Continuous**! Hören Sie danach die Sätze auf der CD und sprechen Sie nach!*

1. (she/wait) *She is waiting.*
2. (I/drink) ____

3. (they/talk) ______________________________

4. (we/meet) ______________________________

5. (he/call) ______________________________

6. (we/sit/in a café) ______________________________

7. (she/eat/a muffin) ______________________________

ÜBUNG 3:

Hören Sie sich die Zahlen an und sprechen Sie nach!

1-29

20 twenty	26 twenty-six	34 thirty-four	60 sixty	90 ninety
21 twenty-one	27 twenty-seven	40 forty	68 sixty-eight	99 ninety-nine
22 twenty-two	28 twenty-eight	42 forty-two	70 seventy	100 one hundred
23 twenty-three	29 twenty-nine	47 forty-seven	73 seventy-three	$^1/_4$ a quarter
24 twenty-four	30 thirty	50 fifty	80 eighty	$^1/_2$ half
25 twenty-five	31 thirty-one	55 fifty-five	86 eighty-six	

GRAMMATIK

Das Present Continuous

Wenn man über etwas spricht, das gerade passiert, benutzt man **Present Continuous**. Das heißt, eine Handlung ist noch nicht abgeschlossen, sondern dauert noch an.

She's waiting for me heißt, sie wartet gerade in diesem Moment auf mich. Ihr Warten dauert noch an und wird erst dann abgeschlossen sein, wenn ich bei ihr bin.

to be (*am/is/are*) + verb with **-ing**

*I **am** eat**ing**.* *She **is** talk**ing**.* *They **are** laugh**ing**.*

Vergleichen Sie:

***I'm meeting** Elvira for coffee **now**.*

Simple Present wird für wiederkehrende Handlungen und Tatsachen benutzt:

***Every week I meet** Elvira for coffee.*

3.2 AT THE CAFÉ

1-30

I'm drinking my coffee and I'm having a big piece of chocolate cake. Elvira is eating a blueberry muffin.

I tell her about the phone call.

"Maybe it isn't a joke, James," she says. "Maybe you have an enemy."

"I'm a police inspector. Criminals don't like me," I say.

"The police can help you," she says. "But be careful."

Suddenly we hear a woman shout. She stands up.

"Help! My money! My money isn't here!"

Inspector Hudson empfiehlt:

Sicher zählen Sie fleißig alles auf Englisch, was Ihnen im Alltag begegnet. Jetzt können Sie das gleiche mit der Uhrzeit machen: Schauen Sie häufig auf die Uhr und überlegen Sie, wie Sie die Uhrzeit auf Englisch ausdrücken würden!

1-31

ÜBUNG 1:

Hören Sie sich die englischen Ausdrücke an und sprechen Sie nach!
Verbinden Sie die Ausdrücke mit ihrer Übersetzung!

1. ☐ Maybe. — a) Kein Problem.
2. ☐ Yes, please. — b) Hilfe!
3. ☐ Don't worry. — c) Bis später.
4. ☐ Careful! — d) Nein, danke.
5. ☐ Help! — e) Vielleicht.
6. ☐ No, thanks. — f) Ja, bitte.
7. ☐ No problem. — g) Vorsicht!
8. ☐ See you later. — h) Keine Sorge.

Rätselkärtchen

Richtig ✓ oder falsch ×?

	✓	×
40 = fourty	a	o
80 = eighty	c	t

1-32

ÜBUNG 2:

Schreiben Sie die Uhrzeiten auf! Hören Sie danach die Sätze auf der CD und sprechen Sie nach!

1. *It's ten past four.*
2. ______________________

KRIMIVOKABULAR

enemy – Feind(in)
to steal – stehlen
thief – Dieb(in)
theft – Diebstahl

3.  ______________________

4.  ______________________

5.  ______________________

6.  ______________________

7.  ______________________

8.  ______________________

9.  ______________________

10.  ______________________

ÜBUNG 3:

Was haben Sie im Text verstanden? Ordnen Sie die Wörter den Gegenständen zu!

(coffee cup, chocolate, blueberry muffin, chocolate cake, blueberries, sugar)

1. ______________________
2. ______________________
3. ______________________
4. ______________________
5. ______________________
6. ______________________

GRAMMATIK

Das Present Continuous

Verwenden Sie das **Present Continuous** mit Zeitangaben wie ***now***, ***this week***, ***at the moment***.

I'm meeting Sir Reginald now. **nicht:** *I meet Sir Reginald now.*

I'm reading a crime story at the moment. **nicht:** *I read a crime story at the moment.*

Die Uhrzeit

Sie kennen alle relevanten Zahlen, jetzt können Sie sich auch genauer mit der Uhrzeit befassen. Die 30 Minuten **nach** der vollen Stunde sind ***past***, die 29 Minuten **vor** der vollen Stunde ***to***. **Viertel vor** bzw. **viertel nach** heißt ***a quarter to*** bzw. ***a quarter past***.

It's a quarter past ten. Es ist viertel nach zehn.

(!) Auch **halb** ist **nach**! **Halb vier** heißt also ***half past three***.

3.3 AT THE CAFÉ

1-33

Elvira and I stand up.
Then a man shouts.
"My wallet! My wallet is gone!"
"My wallet, too!" says another man.
Everybody is looking in their bags. Five more people's wallets are gone.
Somebody is a thief.
"I'm a policeman," I say. "Nobody can leave this café."
I call Scotland Yard. I need another police officer to help me.
Fifteen minutes later Constable Watson arrives.
We need to get everybody's name and address.
We need to look in everybody's bags for the stolen wallets.
Maybe the criminal is here.

1-34

ÜBUNG 1:

Setzen Sie ***somebody, nobody*** *oder* ***everybody*** *in die Lücken ein! Hören Sie danach die Sätze auf der CD und sprechen Sie nach!*

1. (Jeder) ________________ is talking and laughing.
2. (Niemand) ________________ is leaving the café.
3. (Jemand) ________________ is stealing wallets.
4. (Niemand) ________________ is drinking beer.
5. (Jeder) ________________ is drinking coffee.
6. (Jemand) ________________ is shouting for help.

Rätselkärtchen

Richtig ✓ oder falsch ×?

	✓	×
Hudson's wallet is gone.	i	o
Hudson is a good police officer.	l	m

1-35

ÜBUNG 2:

Bilden Sie die ***Present Continuous*** *Form! Hören Sie danach die Sätze auf der CD und sprechen Sie nach!*

1. I go. *I'm going.*
2. She drives. ________________
3. We look. ________________
4. He eats. ________________
5. They shout. ________________
6. We meet. ________________
7. I steal. ________________
8. You stand up. ________________

ÜBUNG 3:

Geben Sie die digitalen Uhrzeiten wieder!

1. 03:27 *Three twenty-seven.*
2. 09:43 ______
3. 11:26 ______
4. 04:15 ______
5. 12:18 ______
6. 06:30 ______
7. 01:39 ______
8. 07:55 ______

ÜBUNG 4:

Hören Sie zu und schreiben Sie die Uhrzeiten auf! Sprechen Sie nach!

1-36

1. ______
2. ______
3. ______
4. ______
5. ______
6. ______

GRAMMATIK

Everybody, ***nobody*** und ***somebody*** stehen immer in der Einzahl:

Everybody is *drinking coffee.*	**Jeder** trinkt Kaffee.
Nobody knows *Elvira.*	**Niemand** kennt Elvira.
Somebody steals *wallets.*	**Jemand** stiehlt Brieftaschen.

Gone ist das **Partizip II** zu ***go***. In diesem Zusammenhang bedeutet *My money is gone*: Mein Geld ist weg – auch wenn das Geld nicht selbst weggegangen ist.

Uhrzeit

Man kann die Uhrzeit auch „digital" ausdrücken.

A quarter to two. = *One forty-five.*
Half past four. = *Four thirty.*
A quarter past seven. = *Seven fifteen.*

! Der Zusatz ***o'clock*** wird nur bei vollen Stunden verwendet, also z.B. bei 8.00 = *Eight o'clock.*

1-37

Constable Watson gets everyone's name and address.
We look in people's bags. We can't find the stolen wallets.
"Shall we go?" I say.
"Okay," replies Elvira.
Elvira and I are walking to our cars.
"I feel bad," I say. "I'm a police inspector. I solve crimes.
But there is a crime here and I can't solve it."
Elvira gets into her red car. She opens the window.
"Don't worry, James. You're a good police officer,"
she says. "You can't work all the time."

Rätselkärtchen

Every wallet ________ gone.
a is **e** are

Five wallets ________ gone.
f is **t** are

1-38

ÜBUNG 1:

Hören Sie zu und setzen Sie die fehlenden Begriffe ein!
(go, loud, shall, Wednesday, going, Sunday, I can't, Saturday, shopping)

"(1.) ____________ we meet next week for coffee?" Hudson asks.

"When?"

"12.30 on (2.) ____________?"

"Sorry, I can't," Elvira says. "Victor and I (3.) __________ to a concert every Wednesday."

"Shall we meet on (4.) ______________?"

"Sorry, I can't. Victor and I go (5.) ______________ on Saturday."

"(6.) ______________ ?"

"(7.) ______________," she says. "Victor and I are (8.) ______________ to a museum on Sunday."

She drives off.

"Victor!" Hudson says in a (9.) ____________ voice.

"I don't like Victor!"

Inspector Hudson empfiehlt:

Lassen Sie sich nicht entmutigen, wenn Sie nicht alles sofort verstehen. Konzentrieren Sie sich auf das Wesentliche. Unbekanntes lässt sich oft aus dem Kontext erschließen.

ÜBUNG 2:

Beantworten Sie die folgenden Fragen mit ***Yes, they can*** *oder* ***No, they can't****!*

1. Can they find the stolen wallets? ____________________
2. Can they get everyone's name and address? ____________________
3. Can they meet for coffee on Wednesday? ____________________
4. Can they find the thief? ____________________
5. Can they solve crimes? ____________________

ÜBUNG 3:

Sehen Sie sich das Bild an und beantworten Sie die Fragen mit ***Yes, it is*** *oder* ***No, it isn't****!*

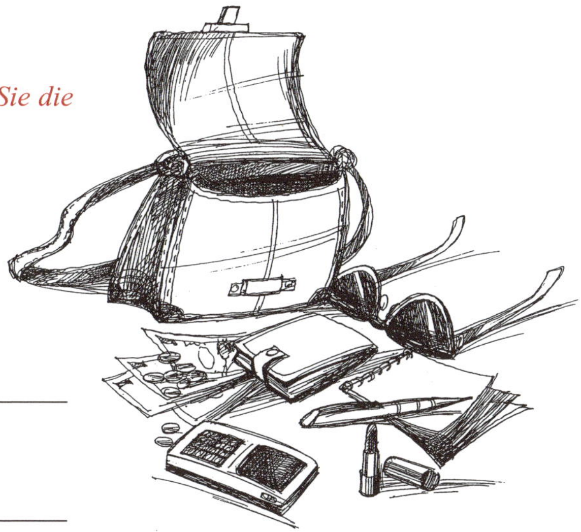

1. Is the wallet gone?

____

2. Is this Hudson's bag?

____

3. Is this a woman's handbag?

____

GRAMMATIK

Oft braucht man einen Textzusammenhang, um ein Wort einer bestimmten Wortart zuordnen zu können.

Z. B. kann **open** sowohl ein Verb als auch ein Adjektiv sein:

*Elvira **opens** the window.*	Elvira öffnet das Fenster.
*The door is **open**.*	Die Tür ist offen.

Phone kann ein Substantiv oder ein Verb sein:

*The **phone** rings.*	Das Telefon klingelt.
*Miss Paddington **phones** Hudson.*	Miss Paddington ruft Hudson an.

Present Continuous und Simple Present

Eine Handlung, die im Moment stattfindet, wird im **Present Continuous** dargestellt. Allgemein wiederkehrende Handlungen stehen im **Simple Present**.

*I'm **drinking** tea.*	In diesem Moment trinke ich gerade Tee.
*I **drink** tea.*	Ich trinke im Allgemeinen Tee; ich mag Tee.

! Gefühle und Sinneseindrücke können nicht im **Present Continuous** stehen:

*I **like** coffee.*	Ich mag Kaffee.	*I **see** you.*	Ich sehe dich.
*He **hears** me.*	Er hört mich.	*The flower **smells** good.*	Die Blume riecht gut.

ÜBUNG 1:

*Markieren Sie die Sätze im **Present Continuous**!*

1. ☐ a) Elvira is eating a blueberry muffin. ☐ b) Elvira eats a blueberry muffin.
2. ☐ a) I'm drinking tea. ☐ b) I drink tea.
3. ☐ a) A woman shouts. ☐ b) A woman is shouting.
4. ☐ a) We're meeting in a nice café. ☐ b) We meet in a nice café.
5. ☐ a) Every week we go to the cinema. ☐ b) Tonight we're going to the cinema.
6. ☐ a) Somebody steals wallets. ☐ b) Somebody is stealing wallets.

ÜBUNG 2:

Ordnen Sie die Wörter zu sinnvollen Sätzen!

1. phone Hudson gets Inspector calls strange

____

2. meeting he Elvira is café at a

____

3. Victor the inspector solve wants help crimes to

____

4. week meet for Elvira I every coffee

____

5. stealing somebody is wallets

____

6. need we get names everybody's to addresses and

____

ÜBUNG 3:

Tragen Sie die korrekte Übersetzung ein und finden Sie das Lösungswort!

1. stehlen _ ☐ _ _ _
2. Hilfe ☐ _ _ _
3. Verbrecher _ _ _ _ ☐ _ _ _
4. Feind _ _ ☐ _ _
5. vorsichtig _ _ _ _ ☐ _ _

Lösung: _ _ _ _ _

Rätselkärtchen

Ist der folgende Satz grammatikalisch richtig?

He is liking tea. ✓ a ✗ e

Lösungswort für Lektion 3: _ _ _ _ _ _ _ _ _ _

Die Vokabelkärtchen gibt es auf **www.lernkrimi.de**

Das Verb

Anders als im Deutschen kann man im Englischen Verben nicht an einer bestimmten Endung (wie **-en** im Deutschen) erkennen. Wenn Sie gut aufgepasst haben, sollte die folgende Übung keine große Hürde für Sie darstellen.

ÜBUNG 4:

Ordnen Sie die Wörter der richtigen Wortart zu!

1. read, car, red
2. loud, like, concert
3. wallet, shout, nice
4. quiet, address, see
5. thief, drive, good

	Verb	Adjektiv	Substantiv
1.	______	______	______
2.	______	______	______
3.	______	______	______
4.	______	______	______
5.	______	______	______

Die Zahlen

Ab 20 werden die Zahlen immer gleich gebildet, genau andersherum als im Deutschen. **Ein**undzwanzig heißt also *twenty-**one***.

! Beachten Sie die Schreibweise!

thirty ***forty*** ***fifty***

WIEDERHOLUNG 1

In dieser Lektion haben Sie die Möglichkeit das Gelernte noch einmal zu vertiefen. Ärgern Sie sich nicht, wenn Sie ab und zu etwas nachschlagen müssen: Auf diese Art erfahren Sie, wo noch eventuelle Schwachpunkte liegen, die Sie dann gezielt beseitigen können.

ÜBUNG 1:

Beantworten Sie die Fragen über sich selbst!

1. What is your name? ______________________________
2. Where do you work? ______________________________
3. What do you do? ______________________________
4. What is your address? ______________________________

ÜBUNG 2:

Setzen Sie die korrekten Possessivpronomen ein!

1. That is __________ book. (I)
2. Victor is __________ friend. (she)
3. Where is __________ mobile phone? (you)
4. Please come to __________ party! (we)
5. That's __________ house. (they)
6. What is __________ phone number? (he)

ÜBUNG 3:

Bringen Sie die nachfolgenden Sätze in die richtige Reihenfolge, so dass das Gespräch einen Sinn ergibt!

1. I'm a policeman.
2. Hello. How are you?
3. Nice to meet you, Victor. My name's James.
4. Good, thanks. And you?
5. Nice to meet you, James. What do you do?
6. Fine thanks. This is my friend Victor.

Lösung: __ __ __ __ __ __

ÜBUNG 4:

Verbinden Sie die englischen Sätze mit ihrer deutschen Übersetzung!

1. ☐ Two letters and a bill.
2. ☐ Every morning I drink tea.
3. ☐ Can you help me?
4. ☐ I read the newspaper.
5. ☐ You look like an opera singer!
6. ☐ I like toast with butter.

a) Können Sie mir helfen?
b) Ich lese Zeitung.
c) Ich mag Toast mit Butter.
d) Sie sehen wie eine Opernsängerin aus!
e) Jeden Morgen trinke ich Tee.
f) Zwei Briefe und eine Rechnung.

ÜBUNG 5:

Setzen Sie die passenden Fragewörter ein!
(when, how, who, where, why, what)

1. __________ is calling please?
2. __________ shall we meet? – There's a nice café on Castle Street.
3. __________ shall we meet? – I'm free at 3.30.
4. __________ are you here? It's Saturday!
5. __________ did the caller say?
6. __________ are you?

ÜBUNG 6:

Schreiben Sie die Sätze im ***Simple Past****!*

1. Who is that? ____________________
2. What do you do? ____________________
3. Where are they? ____________________
4. I am at the office. ____________________
5. Elvira is at home. ____________________

ÜBUNG 7:

Schreiben Sie die Zahlen aus!

1. 6 ______________
2. 11 ______________
3. 38 ______________
4. 20 ______________
5. 4 ______________
6. 12 ______________
7. 100 ______________
8. 14 ______________
9. 43 ______________
10. 99 ______________
11. 70 ______________
12. 51 ______________

ÜBUNG 8:

Schreiben Sie einen Telefondialog zwischen Hudson und Elvira. Benutzen Sie Lektion 2, wenn Sie Hilfe brauchen!

Inspector Hudson: **Hello, Inspector Hudson speaking.**
Elvira: ______________________________
Inspector Hudson: ______________________________
Elvira: ______________________________
Inspector Hudson: ______________________________
Elvira: ______________________________
Inspector Hudson: ______________________________
Elvira: ______________________________
Inspector Hudson: ______________________________
Elvira: ______________________________

ÜBUNG 9:

Schreiben Sie die Uhrzeit auf!

1.  ____________________
2. 09:43 ____________________
3. 01:39 ____________________
4.  ____________________
5. 07:55 ____________________
6. 06:30 ____________________
7.  ____________________
8. 12:18 ____________________
9.  ____________________
10.  ____________________

ÜBUNG 10:

*Markieren Sie die Sätze im **Present Continuous**!*

1. ☐ a) Elvira eats a cake. ☐ b) Elvira is eating a cake.
2. ☐ a) I wait for her. ☐ b) I'm waiting for her.
3. ☐ a) We are going to the cinema. ☐ b) We go to the cinema every week.
4. ☐ a) I read a crime story. ☐ b) I'm reading a crime story.
5. ☐ a) They drink coffee. ☐ b) They are drinking coffee.
6. ☐ a) Everyone is talking and laughing. ☐ b) Everyone talks and laughs.

ÜBUNG 11:

Lesen Sie das Gespräch zwischen Inspector Hudson und dem Kellner und setzen Sie die fehlenden Begriffe ein!

Waiter: Hello. (1.) ________ can I get you?

Inspector Hudson: (2.) __________ a cup of tea, please.

Waiter: Black, or (3.) _________ milk?

Inspector Hudson: With milk, please.

Waiter: (4.) __________ else?

Inspector Hudson: No, thanks. (5.) __________ much is that?

Waiter: That's one pound seventy-five, (6.) __________.

ÜBUNG 12:

Geben Sie die richtige Zeitform an!

1. We're drinking coffee. *Present Continuous*
2. Who was it? __________________________
3. I work for Scotland Yard. __________________________
4. She's calling Inspector Hudson. __________________________
5. I'm meeting a friend in a café. __________________________
6. They were at home on Saturday. __________________________

Jetzt können Sie ...

- sich vorstellen.
- Ihren Beruf sagen.
- eine andere Person vorstellen.
- die Wochentage sagen.
- Objekte einer Person zuordnen.
- Wörter buchstabieren.
- sagen, ob Sie etwas können oder mögen.
- sagen, ob Sie etwas nicht können oder mögen.
- den unbestimmten und den bestimmten Artikel verwenden.
- telefonieren.
- sich höflich ausdrücken.
- Fragen stellen.
- sich in der Vergangenheitsform ausdrücken.
- Anweisungen geben.
- eine Bestellung in einem Café aufgeben.
- bis 100 zählen.
- die Uhrzeit sagen.
- um Hilfe rufen.

4.1 SHOPPING

1-39

At 1.30 p.m. on Saturday, Miss Paddington and I are on Oxford Street. We are shopping for a new winter coat.
"I don't want a new coat," I say.
"Yes, but you need one," says Miss Paddington. "A warm coat."
We go into a men's clothes shop.
Miss Paddington is happy.
Shopping is one of her hobbies.
"There are lots of coats here!" she says. "Perhaps you can find a new hat, too."
The shop assistant is a young man.
He comes over to us.

1-40

ÜBUNG 1:

Hören Sie zu und setzen Sie die fehlenden Begriffe ein!
(mother, sorry, help, size, thank you, customer)

Shop Assistant: Can I (1.) ______________ you?

Inspector Hudson: No, (2.) __________________.

Miss Paddington: Yes! We're looking for a winter coat.

Shop Assistant: What size are you, sir? 42?

Miss Paddington: No, he's a (3.) ___________ 44.

Shop Assistant: Your (4.) _____________ knows all about you!

Miss Paddington: Mother! I'm not his mother!

Shop Assistant: I'm (5.) ________________, your wife.

Inspector Hudson: She's not my wife!

Shop Assistant: I'm so sorry, sir. I'll go and help

that other (6.) ____________________ now.

Rätselkärtchen

Richtig ✓ oder falsch ×?

	✓	×
Hudson likes his old coat.	m	r
Miss Paddington is Hudson's mother.	u	y

ÜBUNG 2:

Hören Sie sich die Aussprache der folgenden Wörter an und sprechen Sie nach! Verbinden Sie die Wörter mit ihrer Übersetzung!

1-41

1. ☐ trousers	a) Hemd	5. ☐ hat	e) Kleid
2. ☐ coat	b) Rock	6. ☐ shirt	f) Schuhe
3. ☐ tie	c) Krawatte	7. ☐ dress	g) Hut
4. ☐ skirt	d) Hose	8. ☐ shoes	h) Mantel

ÜBUNG 3:

Setzen Sie die fehlenden Begriffe ein! Hören Sie danach den Text auf der CD!
(criminal, hat, steal, silly, ties, black)

1-42

"Look at that other customer," Miss Paddington says. "He has a nice (1.) __________ coat. His (2.) __________ and scarf look good, too." The other customer is looking at (3.) __________. All his clothes are black.

"That customer looks like a (4.) ____________ to me," I say. "He might (5.) __________ those ties. Keep an eye on him, Miss Paddington!"

"Don't be (6.) __________," she says. "Crime doesn't follow you everywhere, Inspector!"

KRIMIVOKABULAR

evidence – Beweis
to follow – (ver)folgen
mysterious – rätselhaft

GRAMMATIK

Das Verb in der 3. Person Singular

In der **3. Person Singular** (*he/she/it*) müssen wir ein **-s** an das Verb anhängen.

*I **like** the hat. He **likes** the hat.*
*Inspector Hudson **likes** his old coat.*
*Miss Paddington **likes** the new coat.*

! Endet das Verb auf ***-o*** (*to go, to do*) wird ein ***-es*** angehängt.

! Das Verb ***have*** ändert seine Form und wird zu ***has***.

1-43

Miss Paddington and I leave the shop.
"Let's look in another shop," I say.
"Yes, let's go to Harrods!" says Miss Paddington.
"Harrods is too big for me," I reply. "I don't like big shops!"
We go into a small shop. It has men's and women's clothes.
I see a nice brown coat. It looks like my old coat.
"This one is perfect," I say to Miss Paddington.
"I don't like it," she says.
Suddenly my mobile phone rings.
"Hello, Hudson speaking," I say.
"Hello Inspector," a man says. It's the mysterious caller.
"Who are you?" I ask.
"Nobody," he says. "But I'm watching you, Inspector. I'm watching you right now." He hangs up.

Rätselkärtchen

Hudson has ______ old coat.
[t] a [s] an

He likes ______ brown coat.
[t] a [z] an

Inspector Hudson empfiehlt:

Haben Sie schon einmal darauf geachtet, von wie vielen englischen Wörtern Sie täglich umgeben sind? „Shop" ist Ihnen sicher schon häufig begegnet und sicherlich kennen Sie auch die Bedeutung von Wörtern wie „Shopping", „sorry", oder „mobile" aus unserem Sprachgebrauch. Schreiben Sie eine Liste mit englischen Wörtern, die Ihnen im Alltag häufig unterkommen. Sie werden erstaunt sein, wie viele englische Vokabeln Sie schon kennen! Aber Vorsicht! „Handy" (Mobiltelefon) heißt im Englischen "mobile phone". Das Wort "handy" hingegen bedeutet „handlich, praktisch".

ÜBUNG 1:

Finden Sie die sieben Adjektive in dem Text oben!

1. ______________ (groß)
2. ______________ (klein)
3. ______________ (schön)
4. ______________ (braun)
5. ______________ (alt)
6. ______________ (perfekt)
7. ______________ (geheimnisvoll)

ÜBUNG 2:

Haben Sie verstanden, was der mysteriöse Anrufer gesagt hat? Kreuzen Sie die richtige Übersetzung an!

! Tipp: to watch TV heißt **fernsehen**

"I'm watching you, Inspector. I'm watching you right now."

a) ☐ Ich beobachte Sie, Inspector. Ich beobachte Sie genau jetzt.

b) ☐ Ich fange Sie, Inspector. Ich fange Sie genau jetzt.

ÜBUNG 3:

Sehen Sie sich das Bild an. Beschriften Sie die Gegenstände!
(trousers, coat, dress, shirt, skirt, tie, blouse)

1 ____________
2 ____________
3 ____________
4 ____________
5 ____________
6 ____________
7 ____________

ÜBUNG 4:

1-44

Setzen Sie die gesuchten Begriffe ein! Hören Sie anschließend die Sätze auf der CD und sprechen Sie nach!
(jeweller's, grocery, bookshop, flower shop, furniture shop, bakery, clothes shop)

1. You can buy clothes here. *clothes shop*
2. You can buy flowers here. ____________
3. You can buy jewellery here. ____________
4. You can buy bread here. ____________
5. You can buy food here. ____________
6. You can buy chairs and tables here. ____________
7. You can buy books here. ____________

GRAMMATIK

Let's ist die Kurzform für ***let us*** (lass(t) uns). Es wird verwendet, um Vorschläge zu machen.

like – like

Like kennen Sie schon von Formulierungen wie *I **like** this coat.* ***Like*** kann jedoch noch eine ganz andere Bedeutung haben. Zusammen mit ***look*** bedeutet es **aussehen wie**.

*This **looks like** my old coat.* Der sieht wie mein alter Mantel aus.
*She **looks like** her mother.* Sie sieht wie ihre Mutter aus.

1-45

I look all around. I see people who are shopping. Miss Paddington is talking to a shop assistant.
I go over to her.
"Let's go," I say. "We can't stay here."
"But Inspector," Miss Paddington says. "You need a new coat."
"I like my old coat," I reply. I take her arm. "We're leaving."
We walk towards the exit. Suddenly Miss Paddington stops.
"Look! There's that man with the nice black coat and hat again."
"Where?" I ask. I can't see him.
"Near the ties," she replies.
"Maybe he's buying a tie. Come on."
Just as we are leaving the shop, a man pushes past Miss Paddington. He runs out of the door. It's the man in black.
"My handbag!" Miss Paddington shouts. "That man stole my handbag!"

ÜBUNG 1:

Unterstreichen Sie die richtige Variante!

1. Hudson and Miss Paddington are shop/shopping.
2. They are looking/look at coats.
3. Suddenly the phone ringing/rings.
4. Hudson answers/answering it. It's the mysterious caller.
5. "I'm watch/watching you," he says.

ÜBUNG 2:

Verneinen Sie die Sätze!

1. I say. ______________________
2. You reply. ______________________
3. We run. ______________________
4. They push. ______________________

Rätselkärtchen

Richtig ✓ oder falsch ×?

	✓	×
Hudson and Elvira are shopping.	i	e
Miss Paddington needs a new coat.	p	r

5. He goes. ______________________
6. She leaves. ______________________
7. I kiss. ______________________
8. You speak. ______________________
9. She does. ______________________
10. We catch. ______________________

ÜBUNG 3:

Hören Sie zu und setzen Sie den Satz in die 3. Person Singular!

1-46

1. I say goodbye.

   He ______________________________________

   She ______________________________________

2. You steal my handbag.

   ____

   ____

3. I answer the phone.

   ____

   ____

4. You need a new coat.

   ____

   ____

GRAMMATIK

Verben werden verneint indem man die verneinte Form von **to do** vor das Verb setzt. Das Verb selbst steht bei der Verneinung immer in der Grundform:
*I **do not** answer.*
*She **does not** walk.*

Die Kurzform von **do not** ist **don't**, die von **does not** ist **doesn't.**
*He **doesn't** answer the phone.*
*I **don't go** shopping .*
*Miss Paddington **doesn't** like the old coat.*

1-47

I run out of the shop door. The man is running down Oxford Street.
He has Miss Paddington's handbag.
"Stop, police!" I call out. I start to run. There are too many people on the street. On Saturday, everybody goes shopping.
The man in black is far in front of me. He is too fast. I pull out my mobile phone and call the police. I need backup.

KRIMIVOKABULAR

to catch – fangen
to arrest – festnehmen
suspicious – verdächtig
suspect – Verdächtige(r)

1-48

ÜBUNG 1:

Setzen Sie die fehlenden Begriffe ein! Hören Sie danach den Text auf der CD!
(can't see, too tired, too many, too late, has, don't know)

There are (1.) _______________ people. I can't run fast. The thief is getting away.

I (2.) _______________ what his face looks like. Now I (3.) _______________ him at all.

I can't catch him. It's (4.) _______________. He's gone, with Miss Paddington's handbag.

Miss Paddington runs up. She's got a red face and is (5.) _______________.

"That thief (6.) _______________ all my money, my credit cards and my shopping list," she says. "Crime follows you, Inspector!"

1-49

ÜBUNG 2:

Setzen Sie die fehlenden Begriffe ein! Hören Sie danach die Sätze auf der CD und sprechen Sie nach!
(fast, tired, many, late)

1. I can't catch the thief. He runs too _______________.
2. The man is gone. I'm too _______________.
3. She can't run. She's too _______________.
4. I don't like shopping on Saturday. There are too _______________ people.

Rätselkärtchen

The thief is too _______________.
[i] fast [r] tired

The thief _______________ Miss Paddington's handbag.
[e] have [o] has

ÜBUNG 3:

Miss Paddington ist der Einkaufszettel gestohlen worden. Sehen Sie sich den abgebildeten Zettel an und helfen Sie ihr, die Liste zu vervollständigen! Aber Achtung! Nicht alle der unten aufgeführten Dinge wollte sie wirklich kaufen!
(chocolate, dress, tie, coffee, cake, coat, flowers, tea, newspaper, sugar, milk, muffins)

Inspector Hudson empfiehlt:

Schreiben Sie Ihren nächsten Einkaufszettel so weit wie möglich auf Englisch! So bekommen Sie einen viel direkteren Bezug zu den Begriffen.

GRAMMATIK

Too

Wir benutzen **too** (zu) vor einem Adjektiv, um eine negative Bedeutung hervorzuheben (zu viel, zu groß).

*There are **too** many people.*	Es sind **zu** viele Leute dort.
*The man runs **too** fast.*	Der Mann rennt **zu** schnell.
*This film is **too** scary.*	Der Film ist **zu** furchterregend.

3. Person Singular

Wenn es die Aussprache erfordert – also ein Zischlaut am Ende des Verbs steht – wird in der **dritten Person Singular** ***-es*** statt nur ***-s*** an das Verb gehängt:

*I cat**ch** him.*	–	*He cat**ches** him.*	Ich fange ihn.	–	Er fängt ihn.
*You pu**sh** me.*	–	*She pu**shes** you.*	Du stößt mich.	–	Sie stößt dich.
*I ki**ss** her.*	–	*She ki**sses** me.*	Ich küsse sie.	–	Sie küsst mich.

Like

Die verschiedenen Bedeutungen von ***like*** (***to like*** = mögen, ***to look like*** = aussehen wie) haben Sie bereits kennengelernt. Weitere Bedeutungen finden Sie in Übung 1.

ÜBUNG 1:

Verbinden Sie die englischen Ausdrücke mit ihrer Übersetzung!

1. ☐ I feel like Inspector Hudson.	a) Es sieht nach Regen aus.
2. ☐ I feel like sleeping.	b) Diese Band klingt wie die Beatles.
3. ☐ She is very like her mother.	c) Victor und Elvira sind Gleichgesinnte.
4. ☐ Don't look at me like that!	d) Ich fühle mich wie Inspector Hudson.
5. ☐ Victor and Elvira are like-minded people.	e) Mir ist nach Schlafen zumute.
6. ☐ It looks like rain.	f) Sieh mich nicht so an!
7. ☐ This band sounds like the Beatles.	g) Sie ist ihrer Mutter sehr ähnlich.

Can

Can wird ähnlich verwendet wie das deutsche **können**. Sie können mit ***can*** also eine Fähigkeit ausdrücken.

Farben

Sie kennen die Bezeichnungen für verschiedene Kleidungsstücke, aber kennen Sie auch die Farben? Einige sind Ihnen schon in dieser Lektion begegnet:

*I see a nice **brown** coat.*	Ich sehe einen schönen, **braunen** Mantel.
*It's the man in **black**.*	Es ist der Mann in **Schwarz**.

Für Farbabstufungen benutzt man ***dark*** oder ***light***:

*My skirt is **light** green.*	Mein Rock ist **hell**grün.
*His coat is **dark** blue.*	Sein Mantel ist **dunkel**blau.

ÜBUNG 2:

Verbinden Sie die englischen Farbadjektive mit ihrer Übersetzung. Versuchen Sie, sich an Ähnlichkeiten zu orientieren!

1. ☐ white	a) blau	6. ☐ green	f) orange
2. ☐ red	b) rot	7. ☐ yellow	g) weiß
3. ☐ blue	c) gelb	8. ☐ purple	h) rosa
4. ☐ black	d) grün	9. ☐ orange	i) schwarz
5. ☐ grey	e) lila	10. ☐ pink	j) grau

Direkte und indirekte Rede

Bisher haben Sie Texte in der direkten Rede gelesen. Stellen Sie sich vor, dass Sie bei dem folgenden Gespräch zwischen Miss Paddington und Inspector Hudson dabei waren und Sie Elvira davon berichten.

Beachten Sie:

Aus	*"I don't like big shops," Hudson says.*	"Ich mag große Läden nicht", sagt Hudson.
wird:	*Hudson says that he doesn't like big shops.*	Hudson sagt, dass er große Läden nicht mag.

(!) Vor ***that*** (dass) kommt kein Komma!

Rätselkärtchen

Sind die folgenden Sätze grammatikalisch richtig? ✓ ×

Inspector Hudson don't like shopping. e u

Miss Paddington is happy. s z

Lösungswort für Lektion 4: _ _ _ _ _ _ _ _ _ _

Die Vokabelkärtchen gibt es auf **www.lernkrimi.de**

ÜBUNG 3:

Schreiben Sie den folgenden Text in die indirekte Rede um! Achten Sie auf das -s in der 3. Person Singular!

Miss Paddington: You need a new coat.
Inspector Hudson: I like my coat.
Miss Paddington: It is old. You have to buy a new one.
Inspector Hudson: I don't like shopping.
Miss Paddington: I know a nice big shop.
Inspector Hudson: I don't like big shops.
Miss Paddington: You are impossible!

Miss Paddington says that Inspector Hudson needs a new coat. ____________________

____

____

____

____

____

____

____

____

5.1 BOOKING A HOLIDAY

1-50

Miss Paddington was stressed. We never found her handbag. Elvira was with Victor all the time.
"Go on holiday, Hudson," said Sir Reginald. "You need a break."
I always wanted to go to Edinburgh in Scotland.
Miss Paddington and I sometimes went on holiday together.
"Would you like to go to Edinburgh?" I asked her.
"Wonderful!" Miss Paddington said. She smiled.
She went upstairs to find the suitcases.
I needed to book a hotel. I seldom stayed in hotels.
But I wished to relax.

1-51

ÜBUNG 1:

Hören Sie sich die Aussprache der Häufigkeitsadverbien an und sprechen Sie nach! Verbinden Sie die Wörter mit ihrer Übersetzung!

1. ☐ always	a) selten
2. ☐ never	b) manchmal
3. ☐ often	c) nie
4. ☐ sometimes	d) immer
5. ☐ seldom	e) oft

Inspector Hudson empfiehlt:

Am besten ist es, eine neue Sprache direkt vor Ort zu lernen. Das ist natürlich nicht immer möglich, aber es gibt viele Alternativen. Im Internet kann man englische Zeitungen lesen und sogar englisches Radio hören und auf Englisch fernsehen. Für den Anfang empfehlen sich auch englische Kinderbücher.

ÜBUNG 2:

Finden Sie die Vergangenheitsform der Verben in dem Text oben!

1. is	*was*	4. want	__________
2. find	__________	5. go	__________
3. say	__________	6. aks	__________

7. smile __________ 9. stay __________

8. need __________ 10. wish __________

ÜBUNG 3:

Welche Aussage ist richtig? Markieren Sie mit richtig ✓ oder falsch ✗!

1. Somebody stole Miss Paddington's handbag. ☐
2. Somebody stole wallets at the café. ☐
3. Hudson wanted a new black coat. ☐
4. Hudson always stays in hotels. ☐
5. Elvira's boyfriend is called Victor. ☐
6. Hudson is going on holiday with Elvira. ☐

Rätselkärtchen

Richtig ✓ oder falsch ✗?	✓	✗
Hudson often stays in hotels.	r	s
Sir Reginald needs a break.	e	u

GRAMMATIK

Die Bildung der Vergangenheitsform (Past Tense)

Simple Past wird verwendet, um über Dinge zu berichten, die in der Vergangenheit liegen und abgeschlossen sind. Man benutzt **Simple Past** daher häufig, um Geschichten zu erzählen. Es werden zwei Arten von Verben unterschieden: regelmäßige und unregelmäßige Verben. Bei den regulären Verben wird **Simple Past** dadurch gebildet, dass an die Inifinitivform des Verbes ein ***-ed*** angehängt wird:

work *work**ed***
play *play**ed***
look *look**ed***

Unregelmäßig gebildet werden z. B.:

find ***found***
go ***went***

! Regelmäßig, aber mit unregelmäßiger Schreibung:
say ***said***

Das Häufigkeitsadverb

Das Häufigkeitsadverb steht zwischen dem Subjekt und dem Verb:

I (Subjekt) ***always*** (Adverb) *stay* (Verb) *in hotels.* Ich wohne **immer** in Hotels.

He (Subjekt) ***never*** (Adverb) *drinks* (Verb) *coffee.* Er trinkt **nie** Kaffee.

5.2 BOOKING A HOLIDAY

1-52

Hudson looked on the Internet for "hotel" and "Edinburgh". He found a nice hotel. It was in the centre of Edinburgh. He called the hotel. He wanted a room for himself and a room for Miss Paddington.

Miss Paddington was happy that he used the Internet. Now she did not have to go to a travel agency.

1-53

ÜBUNG 1:

Setzen Sie die fehlenden Begriffe ein! Hören Sie danach den Dialog auf der CD!
(double, non-smoking, name, see you, book, two, arrive, phone number, how many)

Receptionist: Hello, Highland Hotel.

Inspector Hudson: I'd like to (1.) ______________ two rooms, please.

Receptionist: Certainly, Sir. When will you (2.) ______________?

Inspector Hudson: On Saturday.

Receptionist: (3.) ______________ nights?

Inspector Hudson: Four nights.

Receptionist: Would you like (4.) ______________ or single rooms?

Inspector Hudson: (5.) ______________ single rooms, please.

Receptionist: Smoking or non-smoking?

Inspector Hudson: (6.) ______________.

Receptionist: Can I have your (7.) ______________, please?

Inspector Hudson: Of course. It's Hudson, James Hudson.

Receptionist: Thank you. Can I have your (8.) ______________, please?

Inspector Hudson: It's London 555 3696.

Receptionist: Thank you. (9.) ______________ on Saturday, Mr Hudson.

Rätselkärtchen

When will Hudson arrive in Edinburgh?

[i] On Saturday. [a] On Sunday.

How many rooms does Hudson book?

[f] One. [t] Two.

ÜBUNG 2:

Schreiben Sie Ihren eigenen Dialog! Buchen Sie das Zimmer, das Sie möchten! Als Hilfe können Sie den Dialog aus Übung 1 verwenden.

Receptionist: Hello, Highland Hotel.

You: ______________________________

Receptionist: Certainly, Sir. When will you arrive?

You: ______________________________

Receptionist: How many nights?

You: ______________________________

Receptionist: Would you like a double or a single room?

You: ______________________________

Receptionist: Smoking or non-smoking?

You: ______________________________

Receptionist: Can I take your name, please?

You: ______________________________

Receptionist: Thank you. Can I have your phone number, please?

You: ______________________________

Receptionist: Thank you. Goodbye.

You: ______________________________

GRAMMATIK

Die Vergangenheit der unregelmäßigen Verben

Die unregelmäßigen Verben müssen auswendig gelernt werden. Manchmal gibt es jedoch eine kleine Hilfe von den deutschen unregelmäßigen Verben des gleichen Wortstamms, die sich ähnlich verändern:

*f**i**nd*	*f**ou**nd*	f**i**nden	f**a**nd
*d**o***	*d**i**d*	t**u**n	t**a**t
*st**ea**l*	*st**o**le*	st**e**hlen	st**a**hl
*ha**v**e*	*ha**d***	ha**b**en	ha**tt**e

Ohne Hilfe von deutschen Verben:

go	***went***
catch	***caught***
take	***took***

5.3 BOOKING A HOLIDAY

1-54

There are many things to do before a holiday. I have to book a hotel. I have to buy train tickets. I have to pack my suitcase. There's also the rental car to organize. I also have to buy a guidebook about Edinburgh. I always buy guidebooks. There's too much to do!

"Come on, Inspector!" said Miss Paddington. "Let's go to the bookshop for a guidebook."

"Yes," I said. "But I have to call Sir Reginald. Maybe they have found the criminal who stole the wallets. And the thief who stole your handbag."

"Please, don't worry," Miss Paddington said. "Let Sir Reg and Constable Watson solve this crime. We're going on holiday!"

1-55

ÜBUNG 1:

Hören Sie sich die Aussprache der folgenden Wörter an und sprechen Sie nach! Verbinden Sie die Wörter mit ihrer Übersetzung!

1. ☐ rental car	a) Urlaub	5. ☐ room	e) viele
2. ☐ tickets	b) Brieftasche	6. ☐ holiday	f) rauchen
3. ☐ many	c) Zimmer	7. ☐ centre	g) Fahrkarten
4. ☐ to smoke	d) Mietauto	8. ☐ wallet	h) Zentrum

ÜBUNG 2:

Finden Sie die entsprechenden Wörter, die zu den Verben passen!

1. ☐ to pack	a) a hotel	3. ☐ to buy	c) a rental car
2. ☐ to book	b) a guidebook	4. ☐ to organize	d) a suitcase

ÜBUNG 3:

Bilden Sie Sätze über die Dinge, die es noch vor der Reise zu erledigen gibt.

1. (train tickets) ***I have to buy train tickets.***

2. (hotel) ______________________________________

Rätselkärtchen

Richtig ✓ oder falsch ✗? | ✓ | ✗

Miss Paddington wants to buy a guidebook. | c | k

Hudson wants to buy a car. | o | a

3. (rental car) ____

4. (guidebook) ____

5. (suitcase) ____

ÜBUNG 4:

Miss Paddington und Hudson gehen in einen Buchladen. Hören Sie den Text und schreiben Sie die Antworten auf!

1-56

Shop Assistant: Good afternoon. How can I help you?

Miss Paddington: Hello. We're looking for a guidebook about Edinburgh.

Shop Assistant: We have five different guidebooks. This one is very good. It has 340 pages.

Inspector Hudson: (1.) ____

Shop Assistant: This one only has 50 pages.

Miss Paddington: (2.) ____

Shop Assistant: This one is very practical. It has many good tips.

Miss Paddington: (3.) ____

Shop Assistant: This one has a lot of pictures. It costs £30.

Inspector Hudson: (4.) ____

Shop Assistant: Well, this one is small, has some pictures and some tips. It is not very good and it costs only £2.50.

Inspector Hudson: (5.) ____

GRAMMATIK

to have to

Für den allgemeinen Gebrauch des Verbs **müssen** verwendet man das englische **to have to**, das direkt vor das entsprechende Verb gesetzt wird. Hierbei wird **have** konjugiert (*he/she/it has*), das zweite Verb steht im Infinitiv.

*I **have to buy** a coat.*	Ich **muss** einen Mantel **kaufen**.
*She **has to pack** the suitcase.*	Sie **muss** den Koffer **packen**.
*We **have to go** home.*	Wir **müssen** nach Hause **gehen**.

5.4 BOOKING A HOLIDAY

1-57

I went to the train station to book the train tickets. I waited in a queue.
"Hello," I said to the ticket seller. "I'd like two tickets to Edinburgh, please."
"When would you like to travel?" she asked.
"On Saturday," I replied.
"What time?"
"Around 12 midday, please," I said.
"Single or return?"
"Return, please."
The woman put all the information into the computer.
Then she printed the tickets.
"Your train leaves at 12.25 on Saturday," she told me.
"Which platform?" I asked.
"Platform 3," she replied.
I paid for the tickets and thanked the ticket seller.

ÜBUNG 1:

Ordnen Sie die folgenden Verben in die richtigen Spalten ein und geben Sie die Vergangenheitsform an! Handelt es sich um regelmäßige oder unregelmäßige Verben?
(wait, look, am (be), pay, need, find, want, say, are (be), ask, wish, go, put, print, buy)

Regular Verbs		Irregular Verbs	
Present Tense	Past Tense	Present Tense	Past Tense

ÜBUNG 2:

Bringen Sie die nachfolgenden Sätze in die richtige Reihenfolge, so dass das Gespräch einen Sinn ergibt! Hören Sie dann den Dialog auf der CD an!

1-58

1. I'd like a single, please.
2. At 3.30.
3. What time?
4. Hello, I'd like a ticket to London, please.
5. Your train leaves from platform 4 at 3.30.
6. When would you like to travel?
7. Yes, there is a train. Single or return?
8. Thank you.
9. Today.

Rätselkärtchen

Hudson bought two ________ tickets.

[z] single [s] return

Lösung: __ __ 9 __ 2 __ 1 __ __

ÜBUNG 3:

*Schreiben Sie die Gegenwartsform **(Present Tense)** zu den folgenden Vergangenheitsformen auf!*

1. said	________	5. asked	________
2. went	________	6. printed	________
3. waited	________	7. paid	________
4. replied	________	8. thanked	________

GRAMMATIK

Die unregelmäßige Vergangenheit

Wieder sind in der Lektion einige Verben aufgetaucht, deren Vergangenheitsform extra gelernt werden muss:

tell	***told***
buy	***bought***
reply	***replied***
pay	***paid*** (wie *say*)
! *put*	***put***

Das Simple Past

Die am häufigsten verwendete Vergangenheitsform ist das **Simple Past**. Es wird gebildet, indem ein ***-ed*** an den Infinitiv des regelmäßigen Verbs angehängt wird.

! Im **Simple Past** gibt es kein ***-s*** in der 3. Person Singular!

Die unregelmäßigen Verben müssen auswendig gelernt werden. Eine vollständige Liste finden Sie auf den Seiten 138–140.

ÜBUNG 1:

*Schreiben Sie den Text im **Simple Past**! Achten Sie auf die unregelmäßigen Verben!*

Miss Paddington and Inspector Hudson want to go to Edinburgh. They have to book a hotel. They have to buy train tickets. Inspector Hudson finds a hotel on the Internet. He calls the hotel. He goes to the train station and buys the train tickets. They pack their suitcases. They buy a guidebook. They are very happy.

Miss Paddington and Inspector Hudson wanted to go to Edinburgh. ____________________

____

____

____

____

____

____

ÜBUNG 2:

Schreiben Sie über sich selbst! Wie oft unternehmen Sie die folgenden Dinge?

1. I ______________________ go on holiday.
2. I ______________________ use the Internet.
3. I ______________________ stay in hotels.
4. I ______________________ take the train.
5. I ______________________ drink tea.
6. I ______________________ eat toast with butter.

***To have to* oder *must*?**

Anders als im Deutschen gibt es im Englischen verschiedene Möglichkeiten, eine Verpflichtung auszudrücken.

To have to steht hierbei für eine weniger bindende Verpflichtung als ***must***. Im alltäglichen Gebrauch wird daher ***to have to*** sehr viel häufiger verwendet. ***Must*** findet sich oft in Ge- und Verboten:

*You **have to** read this book. It is really good.*	Du musst (solltest) dieses Buch lesen. Es ist wirklich gut.
*You **must** pay your bills!*	Du musst deine Rechnungen bezahlen! (Rechtliche Verpflichtung)

Noch deutlicher wird der Unterschied in der verneinten Form. Hier steht ***mustn't*** (*must not*) für **nicht dürfen**. Für **nicht müssen** (**nicht brauchen**) wird ***needn't*** (*need not*) oder ***don't have to*** verwendet.

To need heißt **brauchen**.

*You **mustn't** steal!*	Du darfst nicht stehlen!
*You **needn't** buy a new coat.*	Du brauchst keinen neuen Mantel zu kaufen.
*You **don't have to** help me.*	Du brauchst mir nicht zu helfen.

ÜBUNG 3:

Setzen Sie die richtige Übersetzung der Verben in Klammern ein!

I (1. muss) ____________________ buy a train ticket. I (2. brauche) ____________________ a guidebook. I (3. darf nicht) ____________________ forget to pack my suitcase. Miss Paddington (4. muss) ____________________ help me. I (5. brauche nicht) ____________________ book a hotel. I (6. muss) ____________________ sleep in a youth hostel. Luckily, I (7. brauche nicht) ____________________ sleep in a tent.

Rätselkärtchen

Ist der folgende Satz grammatikalisch richtig? ✓ ×

Miss Paddington buyed a guidebook. r e

Lösungswort für Lektion 5: _ _ _ _ _ _ _ _

Die Vokabelkärtchen gibt es auf **www.lernkrimi.de**

GOING ON HOLIDAY

1-59

On Saturday James and I arrived at Euston Train Station at 12.10.
We went to platform 3.
The train was there. We got on the train and put our suit-cases in the luggage rack.
Then we found our reserved seats.
The seats were big and we had a table.
I was hungry.

ÜBUNG 1:

*Suchen Sie die neun Verben im **Past Tense** aus dem obigen Text heraus! Geben Sie das **Simple Present** an!*

1. ________________ ________________
2. ________________ ________________
3. ________________ ________________
4. ________________ ________________
5. ________________ ________________
6. ________________ ________________
7. ________________ ________________
8. ________________ ________________
9. ________________ ________________

1-60

ÜBUNG 2:

Hören Sie zu und setzen Sie die fehlenden Begriffe ein!
(opened, drank, said, started, took)

"This is nice," (1.) ______________ Miss Paddington. She opened her new handbag and (2.) ______________ out three magazines. She took out crisps and a thermos of tea. She (3.) ______________ the tea. She (4.) ______________ the crisps and started to eat. She opened a magazine and (5.) ________________ to read.

"Miss Paddington, we are still at Euston Station," I said.

"I know," she said. "I have cake, too!"

ÜBUNG 3:

Hören Sie sich die Aussprache der folgenden Wörter an und sprechen Sie nach! Verbinden Sie die Wörter mit ihrer Übersetzung!

1-61

1. ☐ magazine	a) Zeitung
2. ☐ book	b) Reiseführer
3. ☐ tea	c) Regenschirm
4. ☐ apple	d) Buch
5. ☐ guidebook	e) Chips
6. ☐ newspaper	f) Sandwich
7. ☐ crisps	g) Tee
8. ☐ mobile phone	h) Zeitschrift
9. ☐ sandwich	i) Apfel
10. ☐ umbrella	j) Handy

Rätselkärtchen

What does Miss Paddington eat?

[i] chips [g] crisps

Where starts the train journey of Hudson and Miss Paddington?

[r] Euston Station [t] Edinburgh Station

ÜBUNG 4:

Sind die folgenden Gegenstände zählbar oder nicht? Setzen Sie ***a, an*** *oder – vor die folgenden Substantive!*

1. ______ newspaper	6. ______ crisps
2. ______ umbrella	7. ______ sugar
3. ______ tea	8. ______ milk
4. ______ apple	9. ______ handbag
5. ______ mobile phone	10. ______ sandwich

GRAMMATIK

Zählbar oder nicht zählbar?

Wenn man von einem Gegenstand ein oder mehrere Exemplare zählen kann (z. B. *one magazine, two magazines*), verwendet man die Artikel *a* oder *an*. Verwenden Sie bei nicht zählbaren Substantiven keinen Artikel. Es heißt also nicht: *one milk, two milks*, sondern: *milk*.
Eine Packung bzw. eine Flasche Milch bezeichnet man im Englischen mit "*a packet/bottle of milk*".

6.2 GOING ON HOLIDAY

1-62

I look in my guidebook. There are a lot of interesting places in Edinburgh. There is an old castle. There are a lot of old shops. There are galleries and museums.
I want to go to the medical school and the graveyard. There was a famous case in Edinburgh. In the nineteenth century two men called Burke and Hare stole dead bodies from the graveyard. The "bodysnatchers" sold the bodies to the medical school. Medical students used the bodies for research. My guidebook says I can go on a Murder and Mystery tour of Edinburgh. Tourists can find out about murders and ghosts. Edinburgh is an exciting city.

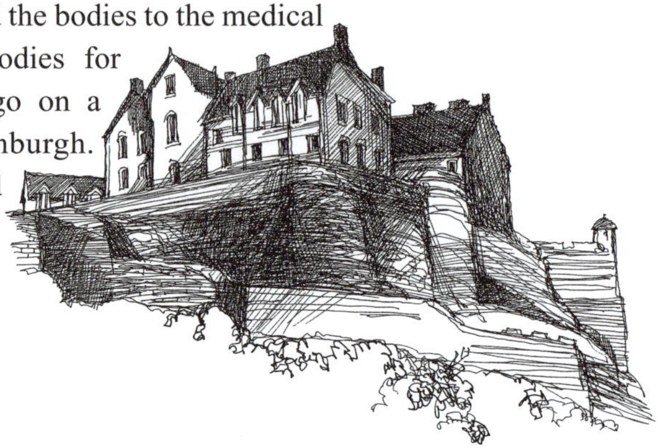

ÜBUNG 1:

Geben Sie die Pluralform an!

1. book	____________	6. robbery	____________
2. body	____________	7. policeman	____________
3. school	____________	8. information	____________
4. leaf	____________	9. story	____________
5. sandwich	____________	10. castle	____________

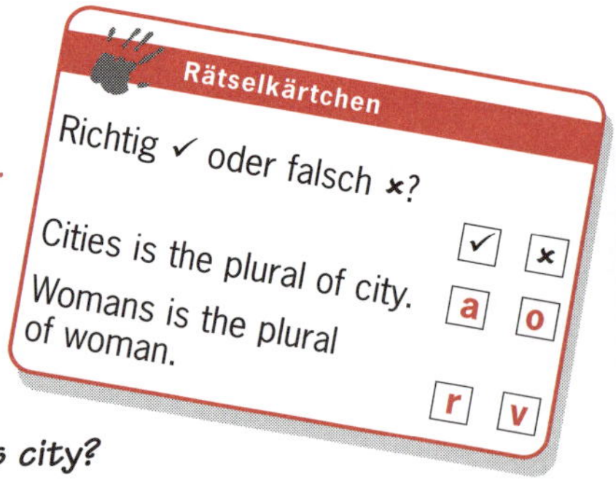

1-63

ÜBUNG 2:

*Bilden Sie Fragen und verwenden Sie dabei die Wörter in Klammern sowie **Is there** oder **Are there any** + **in**! Hören Sie danach die Fragen auf der CD und sprechen Sie nach!*

1. (museums/this city) ***Are there any museums in this city?***
2. (a sandwich/your handbag) ____________________________
3. (toilets/in this building) ____________________________
4. (a castle/Edinburgh) ____________________________
5. (an art gallery/your town) ____________________________

ÜBUNG 3:

Hören Sie zu und setzen Sie die fehlenden Begriffe ein! Sprechen Sie nach!

1-64

Where do you want to go, Inspector?

1. I want to __________ Edinburgh.
2. I want to __________ the medical school.
3. I want to ____________________ the bodysnatchers.
4. I want to __________ the graveyard.
5. I want to __________ the castle.

KRIMIVOKABULAR

bodysnatcher – Leichenräuber
robbery – Raub
robber – Räuber
to rob – rauben

GRAMMATIK

Der unregelmäßige Plural

Die meisten Pluralformen werden mit der Endung **-s** gebildet.
Es gibt aber Ausnahmen: Wenn ein Wort mit ***-ch*** endet (z. B. *watch* – Uhr), endet der Plural mit ***-es*** (z. B. *watches*).
Wenn ein Wort mit ***-y*** endet (z. B. *gallery*), verschwindet das ***-y*** im Plural und wird durch ***-ies*** ersetzt (z. B. *galleries*).
Wenn ein Wort mit ***-f*** endet (z. B. *thief*), verschwindet das ***-f*** im Plural und wird durch ***-ves*** ersetzt (z. B. *thieves*).
Einige englische Substantive besitzen keine Pluralform, z. B. *information* oder *knowledge*.

(!) Die Wörter ***man*** und ***woman*** ändern im Plural ihre Form und werden zu ***men*** und ***women***.

Die Singular- und Pluralformen bei Fragen

Fragen werden durch Umstellung der Aussageformen *There is …* (Singular)/*There are …* (Plural) = Es gibt … gebildet.
Fragen: *Is there/Are there …?* = Gibt es …?
Is there a museum (Singular) *in the city?*
Are there any ghosts (Plural) *in this house?*

1-65

We arrived in Edinburgh in the evening. We took a taxi from the train station to our hotel. We went inside.

"Hello," said the receptionist.

"Hello," I said. "We have a reservation. My name is Hudson."

The receptionist looked at her computer.

"Yes, here it is," she said. "Two rooms, non-smoking. You are in rooms 214 and 215."

"What time is breakfast?" Miss Paddington asked.

"From 7 to 9.30," the receptionist answered.

ÜBUNG 1:

Verbinden Sie die passenden Fragen und Antworten!

1. ☐ What time is breakfast?
2. ☐ Which room am I in?
3. ☐ Do you have a restaurant here?
4. ☐ Do you want smoking or non-smoking rooms?
5. ☐ Do you have a reservation?

a) You are in room 214.
b) Yes, I do, and my name is Hudson.
c) Non-smoking, please.
d) From 6.30 to 9 a.m.
e) Yes, dinner is from 6 to 10 p.m.

Rätselkärtchen

Richtig ✓ oder falsch ×?

	✓	×
Breakfast is from 7 to 9.	u	e
Hudson and Miss Paddington took a taxi from the station to the hotel.	y	w

ÜBUNG 2:

Setzen Sie die für Sie richtigen Zeiten ein!

1. I work from __________ to __________.
2. I watch the news from __________ to __________.
3. I have lunch break from __________ to __________.
4. I go to the gym from __________ to __________.
5. I read the newspapers from __________ to __________.

1-66

ÜBUNG 3

Hören Sie zu und setzen Sie die fehlenden Begriffe ein!
(left, on, excuse me, end, go, here, right)

"(1.) ______________, how can I get to the castle?" Hudson asked the receptionist. She gave him a small map.

"(2.) _______________ is the hotel," she said. They looked at the map. "(3.) __________ along Queen Street. Take the first (4.) __________. Go straight on North St. David Street. At the (5.) __________ of the street turn (6.) __________, past the Scott Monument. Go along Princes Street. The castle is (7.) __________ the left."

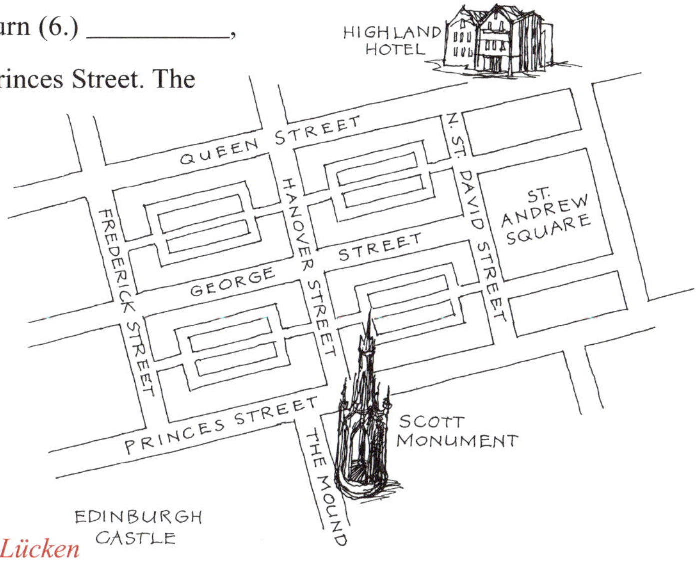

ÜBUNG 4:

Hören Sie sich Übung 3 noch einmal an und zeichnen Sie den Weg vom Highland Hotel zum Schloss in die Karte ein!

ÜBUNG 5:

Setzen Sie die richtigen Wörter in die Lücken ein, um eine Richtung oder Lage anzugeben!
(turn, go straight, at, on, go along, past)

1. ___________ the left.
2. ___________ the end of the street.
3. ___________ the Scott Monument.
4. ___________ Queen Street.
5. ___________ on North St. David Street.
6. ___________ right.

GRAMMATIK

Die Präpositionen

Um im Englischen zeitlich **von ... bis ...** bzw. räumlich **von ... nach ...** auszudrücken, verwendet man ***from ... to ...*** (*from London to Edinburgh, from 8 a.m. to 4 p.m.*).

Sorry oder *excuse me?*

Unterscheiden Sie zwischen den beiden Formen ***sorry*** und ***excuse me***. Um auszudrücken, dass Ihnen etwas leidtut, verwenden Sie *sorry*. Verwenden Sie *excuse me*, wenn Sie z. B. nach dem Weg fragen oder an jemandem vorbei möchten.

1-67

Miss Paddington and I went to our rooms. My room was nice. There was a big bed, a desk, a chair, a fridge and a television. There was a kettle, teabags and instant coffee. I looked out of the window. There was a lovely view of the National Portrait Gallery.
First, I want to have dinner, I thought. Second, I want to walk in the city at night. Third, I want to go to bed and sleep well. Tomorrow I want to see the castle and the gallery.
Suddenly, my mobile phone rang.
"James? It's me," said Elvira. "We have a problem. Sir Reginald was attacked. Please come back to London!"

ÜBUNG 1:

Machen Sie einen kurzen Urlaub und bringen Sie dafür die folgenden Abläufe in die für Sie richtige Reihenfolge!
(read a guidebook, buy train tickets, enjoy your holiday, book a hotel, pack your suitcase)

1. First, ______________________________!
2. Second, ______________________________!
3. Third, ______________________________!
4. Fourth, ______________________________!
5. Fifth, ______________________________!

1-68

ÜBUNG 2:

Hören Sie sich die Aussprache der folgenden Wörter an und sprechen Sie nach! Verbinden Sie die Wörter mit ihrer Übersetzung!

1. ☐ left	a) neben
2. ☐ straight on	b) an ... vorbei
3. ☐ right	c) gegenüber
4. ☐ at the end of the street	d) geradeaus
5. ☐ opposite	e) an der Ampel
6. ☐ next to	f) am Ende der Straße
7. ☐ at the lights	g) durch
8. ☐ diagonally opposite	h) rechts
9. ☐ past	i) links
10. ☐ through	j) schräg gegenüber

ÜBUNG 3:

Setzen Sie die korrekten Präpositionen ein! Hören Sie sich danach den Text auf der CD an!

1-69

Inspector Hudson and I got our suitcases. We went (1.) ____________ the stairs and (2.) __________ the door. We got into a taxi. The taxi drove (3.) ___________ the city to the main station. We went (4.) ____________ the station and I bought two train tickets (5.) ________ London. Then we got (6.) __________ the train. It was a long trip. We arrived (7.) ________ London at 3 a.m. I went home and Hudson went (8.) ____________ his office.

ÜBUNG 4:

Setzen Sie die fehlenden Präpositionen ein!

1. We went to Edinburgh ________ Saturday ________ 12.25.
2. Elvira's birthday is ________ the 26th of May.
3. ________ New Year's Eve we went to Brighton.
4. What are you doing ________ the weekend?
5. He was born ________ 1967.
6. The film starts ________ 8 p.m. ________ Tuesday.

Rätselkärtchen

Miss Paddington was born ______ a Sunday.

d at a on

Inspector Hudson went ______ his office.

a at r to

GRAMMATIK

Im Englischen werden die Ordinalzahlen wie folgt gebildet: *first, second, third, fourth, fifth, sixth, seventh, eighth, ninth, tenth.* Aufzählungen können ebensogut mit den entsprechenden Zahlen ausgedrückt werden: *1st, 2nd, 3rd, 4th, 5th, 6th, 7th, 8th, 9th, 10th.*

Temporale Präpositionen (Prepositions of Time)

on	at	in
Days (on Sunday, on Valentine's Day) **Dates** (on the 13th, on the 23rd of December)	**Times** (at 4.30, at 9.45) **Holidays** (at Christmas, at Easter)	**Years** (in 1971, in 2008) **Months** (in June, in January) **Seasons** (in winter, in summer)

! Mit *weekend* kann **on** oder **at** verwendet werden!

Zählbare und nicht zählbare Begriffe

Im Englischen gibt es – wie im Deutschen – viele Begriffe, die nicht zählbar sind. Hierbei handelt es sich oft um Essenszutaten, die keine definitive Menge bilden und deshalb ohne Artikel stehen, z. B. *tea, sugar, coffee.* Im Gegensatz dazu stehen *an apple, a sandwich, a cake.*

In Lektion 3.1 sagt Hudson jedoch: *"Two sugars, please."* Damit sind zwei Stück Würfelzucker gemeint.

Rätselkärtchen

Welcher der beiden Sätze ist grammatikalisch richtig?

Inspector Hudson's birthday is in the 2nd of July. [t]

Elvira's birthday is in May. [d]

Lösungswort für Lektion 6: _ _ _ _ _ _ _ _ _ _

Die Vokabelkärtchen gibt es auf **www.lernkrimi.de**

ÜBUNG 1:

Setzen Sie, wenn nötig, den richtigen Artikel ein!

1. ___________ new handbag of Miss Paddington is very big.
2. She doesn't drink _____________ milk.
3. Sir Reginald eats ____________ sandwich and ______________ apple.
4. He likes ________________ coffee.
5. We're still at ______________ train station.
6. Is there ________________ castle in Edinburgh?

Der Plural

Die meisten Substantive bilden den Plural, indem ein **-s** angehängt wird. Es gibt jedoch einige Ausnahmen, die beachtet werden müssen:

Singularendung	Pluralendung		
-y	-ies	*baby*	*babies*
-f/-fe	-ves	*thief*	*thieves*
-s	-ses	*glass*	*glasses*
-x/-xe	-xes	*six*	*sixes*
-ch	-ches	*church*	*churches*

Einige Substantive bilden keinen Plural, z. B. ***information***, ***furniture*** (Möbel), ***progress*** (Fortschritt). Beachten Sie, dass Sie hier das Verb im Singular verwenden müssen!

(!) ***News*** (Nachricht(en)) ist ebenfalls ein Singularwort!

ÜBUNG 2:

Geben Sie die richtige Plural- bzw. Singularform an!

Singular	*Plural*
1. castle	___________________
2. ___________________	books
3. graveyard	___________________
4. ___________________	stories
5. man	___________________
6. city	___________________
7. dress	___________________
8. mystery	___________________

ÜBUNG 3:

Beschreiben Sie Ihre Stadt! Benutzen Sie ein Wörterbuch und vervollständigen Sie die unten stehenden Sätze!

1. My city/town has a lot of ____
2. There is ____
3. There are ____
4. There is an old ____
5. There is no ____
6. There are no ____

ÜBUNG 4:

Setzen Sie die fehlenden Begriffe ein!

1. I work _____________ 9 a.m. _____________ 5 p.m.
2. My office is (neben) ___________________ the jeweller's.
3. ______________ 8 o'clock, I eat breakfast.
4. I moved (von) ___________________ London (nach) __________________ Brighton.
5. Go (geradeaus) _________________________, turn (rechts) _____________________ at the end of the street, go (vorbei) ____________________ the church. The restaurant is (gegenüber) ___________________.
6. My child was born _________________ 1976.
7. I always go to Spain ____________________ summer.

WIEDERHOLUNG 2

Schon wieder ist ein großer Teil geschafft! Es ist schön, dass Sie weiterhin so fleißig sind. Jetzt haben Sie wieder die Möglichkeit, das Gelernte zu vertiefen und eventuellen Schwachpunkten entgegenzuwirken.

ÜBUNG 1:

Verbinden Sie die englischen Wörter mit ihrer Übersetzung!

1. ☐ shoes	a) Mantel	5. ☐ shirt	e) Hut
2. ☐ dress	b) Rock	6. ☐ skirt	f) Krawatte
3. ☐ tie	c) Schuhe	7. ☐ hat	g) Hose
4. ☐ trousers	d) Hemd	8. ☐ coat	h) Kleid

ÜBUNG 2:

*Schreiben Sie über sich selbst! Benutzen Sie **I like** oder **I don't like**!*

1. ________________ shopping.
2. ________________ black clothes.
3. ________________ hotels.
4. ________________ the English language.
5. ________________ newspapers.
6. ________________ hats.

ÜBUNG 3:

Schreiben Sie die Übersetzungen auf und finden Sie das Lösungswort!

1. groß _ ☐ _
2. handlich, praktisch _ _ ☐ _ _
3. klein ☐ _ _ _ _
4. Verkäufer/in _ _ _ ☐ _ _ _ _ _ _ _ _ _
5. Handy _ _ _ _ _ ☐ _ _ _ _ _
6. perfekt _ _ _ _ _ ☐ _
7. Möbelladen _ _ _ _ _ ☐ _ _ _ _ _ _ _
8. Kleidung _ _ ☐ _ _ _ _
9. Kunde _ _ _ _ _ _ _ ☐

Lösung: _ _ _ _ _ _ _ _ _

ÜBUNG 4:

Setzen Sie die Verben in die 3. Person Singular (he/she/it)!

1. say ____________________
2. work ____________________
3. go ____________________
4. watch ____________________
5. do ____________________
6. kiss ____________________
7. solve ____________________
8. live ____________________
9. catch ____________________
10. drink ____________________

ÜBUNG 5:

*Tragen Sie das **Simple Past** der angegebenen Wörter ein!*

1. The inspector (pay) _______________ for the train tickets.
2. Miss Paddington and I (go) _______________ on holiday.
3. "Two tickets to Edinburgh, please," he (say) _______________.
4. The seats (be) _______________ big and we (have) _______________ a table.
5. Last year we (stay) _______________ in a hotel.
6. Her handbag (is) _______________ stolen!
7. I (live) _______________ in England for five years. Now I live in Scotland.

ÜBUNG 6:

Schreiben Sie über sich selbst! Benutzen Sie die Häufigkeitsadverbien!
(sometimes, never, always, often, seldom)

1. I _______________ drink coffee in the mornings.
2. I _______________ go on holiday in the summer.
3. I _______________ read newspapers.
4. I _______________ use the Internet.
5. I _______________ watch TV in the evenings.
6. I _______________ go to work by car.
7. I _______________ stay in hotels.

ÜBUNG 7:

Bringen Sie die nachfolgenden Sätze in die richtige Reihenfolge, so dass das Gespräch einen Sinn ergibt!

1. Of course. When will you arrive?
2. How many nights?
3. Two nights.
4. Yes, it's Hudson, James Hudson.
5. Hello, Hotel Haggis.
6. Would you like a single room?
7. I'd like to book a room, please.
8. Thank you, Mr Hudson. Goodbye.
9. I'll arrive on Thursday, the 28th of May.
10. Fine. Can I have your name, please?
11. No, a double room, please.

Lösung: __ __ __ *9* __ *3* __ __ __ __ __

ÜBUNG 8:

Setzen Sie die richtigen Präpositionen in die Lücken ein!

1. *on* Wednesday
2. _____ 1995
3. _____ 6.30 p.m.
4. _____ the 16th of November
5. _____ Christmas Day
6. _____ June
7. _____ the weekend
8. _____ Easter
9. _____ summer

ÜBUNG 9:

Geben Sie die korrekte Pluralform an! Achten Sie auf Ausnahmefälle!

1. newspaper ________________
2. burglary ________________
2. thief ________________
4. woman ________________
5. thing ________________
6. holiday ________________
7. gallery ________________
8. watch ________________
9. information ________________
10. day ________________

ÜBUNG 10:

Bilden Sie Sätze mit ***there is*** *oder* ***there are****!*

1. ________________ an art gallery in my town.
2. ________________ sandwiches in my bag.
3. ________________ ghosts in this house!
4. ________________ a man playing the piano.
5. ________________ champagne on the table.
6. ________________ a castle at the end of the street.
7. ________________ toilets in the café.

ÜBUNG 11:

Setzen Sie die fehlenden Begriffe ein!
(up, into (2x), in, next to, left, opposite)

1. We went _________ the museum.
2. The museum is ______________ the train station.
3. At the end of the street, we turned ______________.
4. I went _________ the stairs.
5. The bathroom is ___________________.
6. I got _________ a taxi.
7. They arrived ___________ Edinburgh.

Jetzt können Sie ...

- Kleidung kaufen.
- sagen, was Sie mögen.
- sagen, was Sie nicht mögen.
- Vorschläge machen.
- Vergleiche ziehen.
- Essen kaufen.
- Hotelzimmer buchen.
- Abfahrtszeiten erfragen.
- Fahrkarten kaufen.
- sagen, wie oft Sie etwas tun.
- Bücher kaufen und vergleichen.
- sich über Sehenswürdigkeiten informieren.
- Aussagen über Ihren Wohnort machen.
- nach dem Weg fragen.
- den Weg beschreiben.

AT THE DOCTOR'S

2-1

I went to the hospital. Miss Paddington came with me. We met Elvira in the waiting room. Victor was there too.

"Sir Reginald has a broken leg," said Elvira. "He has a sore arm and an injured knee. He hit his head, too."

Constable Ann Watson came into the waiting room. With her was her colleague PC Daniel Jewell.

"Who found Sir Reginald?" I asked.

"A neighbour found him and called an ambulance," PC Jewell said.

"Did you find any clues?" Elvira asked.

"Only one," he replied. "A black hat. It was on the ground next to Sir Reginald."

Rätselkärtchen

Does Sir Reginald have a broken leg?

f Yes, he does. b No, he doesn't.

Does he have a cold?

h Yes, he does. i No, he doesn't.

ÜBUNG 1:

Sehen Sie sich das Bild an. Beschriften Sie die Körperteile!

(leg, arm, heart, throat, head, stomach, foot, hand, eye, nose, ear, mouth, knee, finger, toe)

2-2

ÜBUNG 2:

Hören Sie sich die Aussprache der folgenden Wörter an und sprechen Sie nach! Verbinden Sie die Wörter mit ihrer Übersetzung!

1. ☐	cough	a) verletzt		6. ☐	stomach	f) Husten
2. ☐	headache	b) Kehle		7. ☐	throat	g) Magen
3. ☐	knee	c) Fuß		8. ☐	foot	h) Kopf
4. ☐	injured	d) Kopfschmerzen		9. ☐	sneeze	i) wund
5. ☐	sore	e) niesen		10. ☐	head	j) Knie

ÜBUNG 3:

Sehen Sie sich die Bilder an und erzählen Sie dem Arzt, was Ihnen fehlt! Hören Sie danach den Text auf der CD und sprechen Sie nach!
(headache, throat, sneezing, cough, running, cold)

2-3

Doctor: How can I help you?
Patient: I have a (1.) ____________.
I have a sore (2.) ____________.
My nose is (3.) ____________.
I have a bad (4.) ____________.
I am (5.) ____________. I have a (6.) ____________.
Doctor: Please take this medicine and stay in bed for two days.

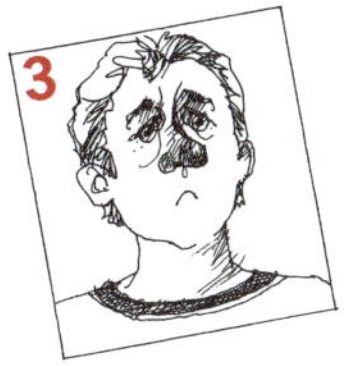

ÜBUNG 4:

Schreiben Sie die richtigen Antworten, indem Sie die entsprechenden Kurzformen verwenden!

1. Did Sir Reginald break his leg? ***Yes, he did.***
2. Did the police find a clue? ________________
3. Did Inspector Hudson stay in Edinburgh? ____________________
4. Did Elvira get attacked? ____________________
5. Did Victor go to Hudson's office? ____________________
6. Did the police find the attacker? ____________________

GRAMMATIK

Die Frage in der Vergangenheit (Past Tense):
Die Fragestellung mit ***to do*** kennen Sie bereits (Unit 2). Möchten Sie eine Frage über die Vergangenheit stellen, setzen Sie das ***do*** ins **Past Tense**:

Do *you* ***see*** *that man?* ***Did*** *you* ***see*** *that man?*

Die Kurzantwort wird nach dem gleichen Schema gebildet:

Yes, I ***do.***	*Yes, I* ***did.***
No, I ***don't.***	*No, I* ***didn't.***

7.2 AT THE DOCTOR'S

2-4

I went into Sir Reginald's room. He was in bed. He had a bandage around his head and his leg was in plaster. He had a drip in his arm. A nurse gave him a drink of water.

"Hello," I said. "You look terrible."

"I know," said Sir Reginald. He tried to smile.

"Please tell me what happened," I said.

"I don't know," he said.

"Did you see the attacker?" I asked.

"No, I didn't. It was dark. I came home. I took my key out of my briefcase. Then a man hit me on the head," Sir Reginald said. He was very tired. He closed his eyes.

"I'm sorry," he said. "I don't remember."

ÜBUNG 1:

Welcher Satz ist korrekt? Kreuzen Sie an!

1. a) ☐ Please tell to me what happened.
   b) ☐ Please tell me what happened.
   c) ☐ Please say me what happened.

2. a) ☐ I know not.
   b) ☐ I don't can know.
   c) ☐ I don't know.

3. a) ☐ Have you see the attacker?
   b) ☐ Did you see the attacker?
   c) ☐ See you the attacker?

4. a) ☐ I don't remember.
   b) ☐ I remember not.
   c) ☐ I don't can remember.

Rätselkärtchen

Richtig ✓ oder falsch ×?

	✓	×
Sir Reginald hit someone on the head.	k	r
Someone hit Sir Reginald on the head.	e	o

ÜBUNG 2:

Welche Aussagen stimmen? Markieren Sie mit richtig ✓ oder falsch ✗!

1. The attacker left a black hat at the scene of the crime. ☐
2. Hudson got a phone call from a strange man. ☐
3. Miss Paddington was attacked. ☐
4. Elvira likes to help solve crime. ☐
5. Victor Crawley works for Scotland Yard. ☐
6. A man in a black coat stole Miss Paddington's handbag. ☐

ÜBUNG 3:

Setzen Sie die fehlenden Begriffe ein!

(went into, waited in, went to, spoke to, lying in)

1. He ________________ the doctor.
2. She was ________________ bed.
3. They ________________ Sir Reginald's room.
4. We ________________ the waiting room.
5. You ________________ the hospital.

GRAMMATIK

Präpositionen

Präpositionen folgen keinen bestimmten Regeln, die man lernen könnte. Man muss sie vielmehr einzeln lernen. Es werden sogar manchmal unterschiedliche Präpositionen im Britischen und im Amerikanischen Englisch verwendet.

In/into oder out/out of

Verwenden Sie ***into*** oder ***out of*** bei einem nachfolgenden Substantiv, wenn die Richtung der Bewegung angegeben wird:

*We went **into** the room.*	Wir gingen **in** das Zimmer.
*We got **out of** the taxi.*	Wir stiegen **aus** dem Taxi **aus**.

Verwenden Sie ***in*** oder ***out***, wenn kein Substantiv folgt, die Information also allgemein gehalten wird:

*We went **in**.*	Wir gingen **hinein**.
*We got **out**.*	Wir stiegen **aus**.

2-5

I was tired.

"I need to go home," I said to Elvira and Victor in the waiting room. "I need food and sleep."

"I'm staying here," said Elvira. "I think I'll stay with Sir Reginald."

"I need to go home, too," said Victor. "But I think I'll come back tomorrow."

"Thank you, Victor," Elvira said. She gave him a kiss. I looked at the painting on the wall.

"I'll take you home," Victor said to me.

"No, no, I'll take a taxi," I replied.

"Please, Inspector," Victor said. "I want to help."

ÜBUNG 1:

Schreiben Sie die richtige Kurzform!

1. I will *I'll*
2. he will ________________
3. she will ________________
4. it will ________________
5. we will ________________
6. they will ________________
7. you will ________________

KRIMIVOKABULAR

crime scene – Tatort
attack – Angriff
attacker – Angreifer(in)
to attack – angreifen
injured – verletzt
clue – Hinweis
victim – Opfer

ÜBUNG 2:

2-6

*Setzen Sie die fehlenden Begriffe im **Simple Past** ein! Hören Sie danach den Text auf der CD!*

Victor and I (1. drive) ________________ back to my house. I thanked him for the ride and (2. shake) ________________ his hand. Then I (3. go) ________________ into the house. I (4. switch) ________________ on the light. There (5. be) ________________ a letter on the table. It (6. have) ______________ my name on it. I (7. open) ______________ it.

Dear Inspector,

You will never find me. You are in danger and your friends are, too. Sir Reginald is in hospital. What will happen to Miss Paddington? What will happen to Elvira? Who will be a victim next? Be careful. I'm always watching you.

ÜBUNG 3:

*Vervollständigen Sie die Sätze mit **I think I'll** und dem Verb in Klammern!*

1. I'm tired. (go) *I think I'll* go home.
2. There is a letter. (open) __________________________ it.
3. I'm hungry. (have) __________________________ a sandwich.
4. It's cold in here. (close) __________________________ the window.
5. Don't drive me home. (take) __________________________ a taxi.

Rätselkärtchen

Victor ________ to help.
[e] wants [a] will

I'm ________ watching you.
[n] always [m] never

GRAMMATIK

Too (auch)
Too steht am Ende des Satzes:
– *I'll have coffee.*
– *I'll have coffee, **too**.*

Will
Um etwas in der Zukunft auszudrücken, kann man **will** verwenden. Meistens wird es zu **'ll** abgekürzt:

*I **will***	***I'll***
*he **will***	*he**'ll***

Wir benutzen **will** um eine Annahme oder Vorhersage über die Zukunft auszudrücken. Es wird dann meistens in Kombination mit ***I think*** oder ***maybe/perhaps*** (vielleicht) verwendet:
***I think I'll** go.*
***Maybe he'll** come, too.*

AT THE DOCTOR'S

2-7

Suddenly, the lights were switched off. I was in the dark. Someone cut the electricity, I thought. Then I heard breaking glass. It was upstairs. Miss Paddington was in bed upstairs. At that moment my mobile phone rang. I didn't want the criminal to know I was downstairs.

I didn't answer it. I went slowly up the stairs. Then I heard Miss Paddington scream. I ran up the stairs and into her room. The curtains were on fire! Miss Paddington was in bed. She was screaming.

"Someone threw a bottle through the window!" she screamed. "It had rags in it and the rags were on fire!"

2-8

ÜBUNG 1:

Verbinden Sie die Fragen mit den richtigen Antworten! Hören Sie anschließend die Sätze auf der CD und sprechen Sie nach!

1. When did you get home?	☐ At 4 a.m.
2. How long were you at home?	☐ A moment ago.
3. What time did you get home?	☐ At 6.30 p.m.
4. How long were you at the hospital?	☐ Twenty minutes ago.
5. When did you hear the phone ring?	☐ For an hour.
6. What time did Sir Reginald get attacked?	☐ For twenty minutes.

ÜBUNG 2:

*Setzen Sie **for**, **ago**, oder **at** in die Lücken ein!*

1. I came home __________ 3 a.m.

2. I was at the party ___________ six hours.

3. Two days ____________, I came home from Edinburgh.

4. I was in Edinburgh _____________ one week.

5. I was on the train _____________ eight hours.

6. ___________ ten o'clock, I was back in London.

Rätselkärtchen

Richtig ✓ oder falsch ×? | ✓ | ×

Miss Paddington was on fire. | k | g

Inspector Hudson threw the bottle. | r | i

ÜBUNG 3:

*Bilden Sie Sätze mit dem **Past Continuous** und **Simple Past**!*

1. Hudson (stand) ***was standing*** downstairs when the phone (ring) ***rang***.
2. They (shop) _______________ for a coat when somebody (steal) _______________ her handbag.
3. He (go) _______________ into the house when he (be attacked) _______________

GRAMMATIK

Das Past Continuous

Das **Past Continuous** wird verwendet, um eine fortdauernde Handlung in der Vergangenheit zu beschreiben, die eventuell durch eine kurze Handlung im **Simple Past** unterbrochen wird:

*Yesterday, I **was reading** a book (, when the phone **rang**).*

Zeitangaben

at

Um einen konkreten Zeitpunkt anzugeben, wird **at** benutzt:

***at** 11.30, **at** midday*

ago

Ago entspricht dem deutschen **vor**:

*I came home ten minutes **ago**.* Ich bin **vor** zehn Minuten nach Hause gekommen.

for

Um den Zeitraum einer Handlung anzugeben, wird **for** verwendet. Es kann mit dem deutschen **lang** übersetzt werden:

*I was in hospital **for** three days.* Ich war drei Tage **lang** im Krankenhaus.

Fragen mit *to do* in der Vergangenheit

Beachten Sie, dass bei Fragen mit ***to do*** nur ***do*** und nicht auch das zweite Verb in die Vergangenheit gesetzt wird:

***Do** you **have** a headache?* ***Did** you **have** a headache?*

ÜBUNG 1:

*Bilden Sie Fragen mit **did** und den Begriffen in Klammern! Geben Sie die Kurzantwort!*

1. (she/meet/Victor)	*Did she meet Victor?*	Yes, *she did*.
2. (Hudson/go/on holiday)	______________________	Yes, __________
3. (I/shut/the window)	______________________	No, __________
4. (you/buy/milk)	______________________	Yes, __________
5. (he/get/the job)	______________________	No, __________
6. (they/feed/the cat)	______________________	No, __________

ÜBUNG 2:

Beschreibung von Schmerzen und Wunden: Verbinden Sie die Wörter mit ihrer Übersetzung!

1. ☐ deep	a) Schmerz	6. ☐ bad	f) Wunde
2. ☐ sharp	b) leicht	7. ☐ pain	g) stechend
3. ☐ throbbing	c) schmerzen	8. ☐ to ache	h) kommt und geht
4. ☐ light	d) wund	9. ☐ wound	i) pochend
5. ☐ comes and goes	e) tief	10. ☐ sore	j) stark

Sinnesempfindungen ausdrücken

Es gibt viele feststehende Ausdrücke für die verschiedenen Sinnesempfindungen. Bei Schmerzen können Sie meist den Ausdruck ***I have a …ache.*** verwenden:

I have a toothache.	Ich habe Zahnschmerzen.
I have a headache.	Ich habe Kopfschmerzen.
I have a muscleache.	Ich habe Muskelkater.

Für Hunger, Durst, Kälte, Wärme usw. gibt es ebenfalls feststehende Wendungen:

I am hungry.	Ich habe Hunger.	*I am sad.*	Ich bin traurig.
I am thirsty.	Ich habe Durst.	*I am cold.*	Mir ist kalt.
I am tired.	Ich bin müde.	*I am hot.*	Mir ist heiß.

(!) *I have a cold* bedeutet, dass ich eine Erkältung habe, nicht, dass mir kalt ist!

Das Past Continuous

Diese Zeitform wird mit der Vergangenheitsform von ***to be*** (*was/were*) + ***-ing***-Form des Verbs gebildet. Sie zeigt eine fortlaufende Handlung in der Vergangenheit an. Wird diese fortlaufende Handlung durch eine weitere, kurze Handlung unterbrochen, steht diese im **Simple Past**:

When we ***arrived*** *at the hospital* (kurze Handlung), *Elvira* ***was waiting*** *for us* (fortdauernde Handlung).	Als wir im Krankenhaus ankamen, wartete Elvira auf uns.
You ***were talking*** *to a man* (fortdauernde Handlung) *when I* ***saw*** *you* (kurze Handlung).	Sie sprachen mit einem Mann, als ich Sie sah.

ÜBUNG 3:

Schreiben Sie die Sätze im ***Present Continuous*** *ins* ***Past Continuous*** *um! Benutzen Sie* ***was*** *oder* ***were****!*

1. The phone is ringing. *The phone was ringing.*
2. Elvira and Hudson are talking. ______________________
3. Miss Paddington is screaming. ______________________
4. The men are talking. ______________________
5. She is waiting at the hospital. ______________________
6. They are going to Edinburgh. ______________________
7. I am reading a thriller. ______________________

ÜBUNG 4:

In welcher Zeitform stehen die Sätze? Verbinden Sie!

1. ☐ I was tired.	a) Present Continuous
2. ☐ I need food.	b) Future
3. ☐ I'm staying.	c) Simple Past
4. ☐ I'll come back.	d) Simple Present

Rätselkärtchen

Sind die Sätze grammatikalisch richtig? ✓ ✗

	✓	✗
I was reading when he attacked me.	n	m
Did you saw the man?	s	e

Lösungswort für Lektion 7: _ _ _ _ _ _ _ _ _ _

Die Vokabelkärtchen gibt es auf **www.lernkrimi.de**

8.1 AT HOME

2-9

"Come on, Miss Paddington!" I shouted. "Get out of bed!" She jumped out of bed. Together we ran downstairs. I picked up the phone and called the fire service.
"Hurry!" I said.
I gave my name and address. Then Miss Paddington and I ran out of the house. We saw the flames from the fire coming out of the bedroom window.
We were standing in the garden when the fire engine came. The firemen put the fire out.
"Who did it?" asked Miss Paddington. She was crying. "Who threw that bottle?"
"I think I know," I said.

Rätselkärtchen

Richtig ✓ oder falsch ×?

	✓	×
Hudson's house is on fire.	k	p
Miss Paddington's bedroom is on fire.	n	l

2-10

ÜBUNG 1:

Setzen Sie die fehlenden Begriffe ein! Hören Sie danach die Sätze auf der CD und sprechen Sie nach!

(on a chair, in the bathroom, in a bed, in the kitchen, in an armchair, in the living room)

1. You sleep ______________________
2. You sit ______________________
3. The armchair is ______________________
4. You cook ______________________
5. When I eat, I sit ______________________
6. You brush your teeth ______________________

ÜBUNG 2:

Verbinden Sie die passenden Begriffe miteinander!

1. ☐ pick up
2. ☐ call
3. ☐ break
4. ☐ look at
5. ☐ give
6. ☐ go
7. ☐ drink

a) a picture
b) a kiss
c) the phone
d) home
e) some water
f) the fire service
g) the glass

ÜBUNG 3:

Bilden Sie einen Satz, indem Sie die Wörter in die richtige Reihenfolge bringen!

1. answer phone I didn't the

____

2. think I I know

___

3. home need go I to

___

4. I remember sorry don't

___

ÜBUNG 4:

Beschriften Sie die Gegenstände!
(bed, chair, armchair, table, sofa, wardrobe)

1. ____________________
2. ____________________
3. ____________________
4. ____________________
5. ____________________
6. ____________________

GRAMMATIK

Das Verb *to think* (denken)

Im Englischen wird ***to think*** häufiger gebraucht als im Deutschen **denken**. Es kann wie im Deutschen benutzt werden, um einen Gedanken auszudrücken:

I think *about him every day.* **Ich denke** jeden Tag an ihn.

Oft wird es aber auch im Sinne von deutsch **glauben** verwendet:

I think *I know who did it.* **Ich glaube**, ich weiß, wer es getan hat.

I think *I'll take the chocolate cake.* **Ich glaube**, ich nehme den Schokoladenkuchen.

Wenn man sich nicht sicher ist:

I think *so.* **Ich glaube** schon.

Außerdem kann man mit ***to think*** seine Meinung ausdrücken:

I think *eating meat isn't right.* **Ich finde** es nicht richtig, Fleisch zu essen.

2-11

An hour later, Miss Paddington and I arrived at Elvira's house. Victor was sitting on the sofa when we went inside.

"You are the man in black." I said to Victor.
"What?" Victor said.
"You were at my house tonight. You threw the burning bottle," I said.
Elvira stood up.
"You're crazy, James," she said. "There is no motive. You can't prove it!"
"You are jealous of me," Victor said, "because Elvira and I are together. I drove away from your house, then I called you. Listen to your mailbox, Inspector. I didn't come back to throw a bottle."

Rätselkärtchen

Miss Paddington ________ the fire engine coming.
o hears   d listen to

________ your mailbox!
z Hear   w Listen to

ÜBUNG 1:

Fügen Sie das richtige Fragewort ein!
(where, why, what, why not, who)

1. – You are the criminal!
   – ____________?
   – You stole the handbag.
2. – I want to go on holiday.
   – _____________?
   – Spain. It's warm there.
3. – I saw somebody today.
   – ______________?
   – My friend Elvira.
4. – I like this book.
   – ______________?
   – Because it's exciting!
5. – I don't like that film.
   – ______________?
   – Because it's boring.

ÜBUNG 2:

Unterstreichen Sie die richtige Variante!

1. Last night we drived/drove to your house.
2. At the moment we talk/are talking.

3. You breaked/broke the glass!
4. They were sat/sitting when we arrived.
5. I thought/thinked it was you!
6. I think I have/will have a drink.
7. I work/am working for Scotland Yard.
8. Miss Paddington was cry/crying.

ÜBUNG 3:

***Listen** or **hear**? Setzen Sie das korrekte Wort ein!*

1. I can ____________ the phone ringing.
2. ____________! Someone is screaming!
3. Please ____________ to me when I'm talking.
4. Please speak louder. I can't ____________ you.
5. Can you ____________ that music?
6. He has to ____________ to his mailbox.

KRIMIVOKABULAR

fire – Feuer
arson – Brandstiftung
motive – Motiv
dead – tot
strangled – stranguliert

GRAMMATIK

Kurzfragen

Um eine kurze Frage zu stellen, können Sie wie im Deutschen das Fragewort allein verwenden:

– *You are the man in black.* – Sie sind der Mann in Schwarz.
– ***What?*** – **Was?**

Auf die gleiche Art können Sie eine negative Frage stellen:

– *I don't like coffee.* – Ich mag keinen Kaffee.
– ***Why not?*** – **Warum nicht?**

To hear und *to listen*

Obwohl beide Verben **hören** bedeuten, werden sie unterschiedlich verwendet. ***To hear*** schließt alle mit dem Hören verbundenen Aktivitäten ein, während ***to listen*** sich nur auf aktives Zuhören beschränkt:

*Inspector Hudson **hears** a scream.*
*I can **hear** the phone ring.*
*I **listen** to the radio.*
***Listen!** Miss Paddington is screaming!*

8.3 AT HOME

2-12

I looked at my mobile. I saw that I had one new message. It came the moment after the window broke.

I called my mailbox and listened to the message. I heard Victor's voice.

"Hello, Inspector. I'm worried. Maybe Elvira is in danger."

Then I heard the sound of a car horn.

"Crazy driver!" I heard Victor say. "Someone nearly hit my car!" Then I heard a strange noise. The phone connection was bad. I heard Victor say: "…no signal… see… hospital." Then he hung up.

I looked at Victor and Elvira. They were sitting together on the sofa.

"Please, Inspector, let me help you," said Victor. "With your police skills and my knowledge of crime, we can find the real criminal."

2-13

ÜBUNG 1:

Setzen Sie die fehlenden Begriffe ein! Hören Sie danach die Sätze auf der CD und sprechen Sie nach!
(at the last moment, the moment after, a moment, at the moment, a moment later)

Rätselkärtchen

He ________ buy a new coat.
[h] must [l] has to

You ________ steal!
[e] must not [u] don't have to

1. The phone rang ________________________ the window broke.
2. I'm not working ________________________. I'm on holiday.
3. We ran down the stairs ________________________.
4. The fire engine came ________________________.
5. Do you have ________________________? We need to talk.

2-14

ÜBUNG 2:

Hören Sie sich den Text an und unterstreichen Sie die Entsprechung des deutschen Verbs ***müssen****!*

Inspector Hudson and I had to stay at Elvira's house. We couldn't go back to Hudson's house. Elvira's insurance company had to investigate the fire because it was arson. We had to clean the house. I had to buy new clothes. At Elvira's house Hudson had to sleep on the sofa in the living room. I slept in the spare bedroom. We had to share one bathroom and the kitchen was very small.

ÜBUNG 3:

Sehen Sie sich den Grundriss an und beschriften Sie die Zimmer!
(living room, bedroom, spare bedroom, bathroom, kitchen, corridor)

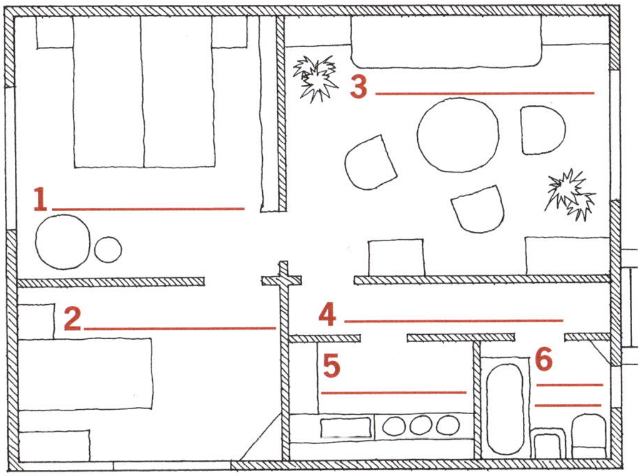

ÜBUNG 4:

*Bilden Sie Sätze mit **to have to** und den vorgegebenen Wörtern!*

1. on Saturday/she/go/shopping. *On Saturday she has to go shopping.*
2. tonight/he/study/English. ____________
3. you/listen to/your mailbox. ____________
4. she/go to/the toilet. ____________
5. they/call/Elvira/at 8 p.m. ____________

GRAMMATIK

To have to und must

Das deutsche Verb **müssen** in der Bedeutung von **sollen** wird normalerweise mit ***to have to*** übersetzt. Das Verb ***must*** hat eine sehr viel stärkere Bedeutung und wird hauptsächlich für Regeln und Verbote verwendet:

You have to *see this film!*	**Du musst (solltest)** diesen Film sehen!
You must *pay taxes.*	**Du musst** Steuern zahlen. (Gesetz)

! In der negativen Form ist der Unterschied noch deutlicher. ***Not to have to*** heißt soviel wie **nicht müssen/nicht brauchen**, während ***must not*** **nicht dürfen** ausdrückt!

*You **don't have to** cook.*	Du **musst nicht/brauchst nicht** zu kochen.
*You **mustn't drink** coffee.*	Du **darfst** keinen Kaffee trinken.

8.4 AT HOME

2-15

On Saturday Elvira came into the living room.
"Victor and I are going on holiday," she said. "We're going to Brighton!"
"That's nice," I replied. "Brighton is wonderful. But please be careful. I don't want you to get hurt."
Later that day I went into my office at Scotland Yard. I looked at my reports. Forensic scientists analysed the black hat clue. They looked for some hairs. They didn't find any because the hat was new. Now the police were trying to find the shop which sold the hat. Maybe the shop assistant would remember who bought it.

KRIMIVOKABULAR

proof – Beweis
to prove – beweisen
hostage – Geisel
to commit a crime – ein Verbrechen begehen

ÜBUNG 1:

Verbinden Sie die Verben mit der passenden Verneinung!

1. ☐ found
2. ☐ going
3. ☐ came
4. ☐ went
5. ☐ bought
6. ☐ trying

a) didn't come
b) didn't buy
c) wasn't going
d) didn't go
e) wasn't trying
f) didn't find

Rätselkärtchen

Richtig ✓ oder falsch ×?

	✓	×
Elvira is going to Brighton.	d	f
Constable Watson is dead.	g	l

ÜBUNG 2:

Lesen Sie den Text noch einmal und übersetzen Sie die Wörter ins Englische!

1. Wohnzimmer ____________________
2. Urlaub ____________________
3. aber ____________________
4. vorsichtig ____________________
5. verletzt ____________________
6. später ____________________
7. Büro ____________________
8. Berichte ____________________
9. weil ____________________
10. Laden ____________________
11. vielleicht ____________________
12. sich erinnern ____________________

2-16

ÜBUNG 3:

Hören Sie zu und setzen Sie die fehlenden Begriffe ein!
(her mobile, a police car, the floor, the investigation, Ann's flat, the living room, not available, to talk)

Constable Watson was working on (1.) ______________________. I wanted (2.) ____________________ to her. I called (3.) ______________________. I got a message saying the number was (4.) ______________________. I had a bad feeling. I left the Yard and got into (5.) ______________________. I drove to Ann's address in High Wycombe. At (6.) ______________________, I knocked on the door. I tried the doorknob. The door opened. In (7.) ______________________, I found Constable Watson. She was lying on (8.) ______________________, dead. She had been strangled.

GRAMMATIK

Die Verneinung im Past Tense

Das Verb ***to do*** hat die unregelmäßige Vergangenheitsform ***did***. Es wird verwendet, um die Verneinung im **Simple Past** zu bilden. Das Hauptverb wird hierbei in den Infinitiv gesetzt:

*He **went** to the cinema.* — *He **didn't go** to the cinema.*

Aus ***did not*** wird ***didn't***.

Im **Past Continuous** wird die Vergangenheitsform vom Hilfsverb ***to be*** verneint. Die ing-Form bleibt erhalten:

*I **was reading** a book.* — *I **wasn't reading** a book.*
*They **were drinking** coffee.* — *They **weren't drinking** coffee.*

Aus ***was not*** wird ***wasn't***, aus ***were not*** wird ***weren't***.

Die Verneinung

Die Verneinung mit ***to do*** im **Past Tense** folgt dem gleichen Schema wie im **Simple Present**:

*He **buys** a book.*	Er kauft ein Buch.
*He **doesn't buy** a book.*	Er kauft kein Buch.
*He **bought** a book.*	Er kaufte ein Buch.
*He **didn't buy** a book.*	Er kaufte kein Buch.

(!) In der verneinten Form steht das zweite Verb im Infinitiv.

Im **Present Continuous** erfolgt die Verneinung nicht mit ***to do***, sondern nur mit ***not***:

*I'**m reading** a book.*	Ich lese ein Buch.
*I'**m not reading** a book.*	Ich lese kein Buch.
*I **was reading** a book.*	Ich las ein Buch.
*I **wasn't reading** a book.*	Ich las kein Buch.

(!) Im Englischen ist "police" ein Pluralwort. Deshalb steht hier das Verb in der Mehrzahl: The police **have** caught the thief.

ÜBUNG 1:

Schreiben Sie die positive bzw. negative Form der Sätze auf!

1. I found Ann Watson. ***I didn't find Ann Watson.***
2. They looked for hairs.

___

3. The police were trying to find the shop.

___

4. Inspector Hudson heard Victor's voice.

___

5. He didn't see me.

___

6. They weren't listening to the radio.

___

7. You aren't a good inspector.

___

8. We were frightened.

___

9. She's not a housekeeper.

____

10. Elvira didn't like tea.

____

ÜBUNG 2:

Verbinden Sie die Wörter mit ihrer Übersetzung!

1. ☐	carpet	a) Glas	9. ☐	glass	i) Fenster
2. ☐	window	b) Herd	10. ☐	freezer	j) Toilette
3. ☐	flat	c) Dusche	11. ☐	fork	k) Löffel
4. ☐	shelf	d) Teller	12. ☐	basin	l) Teppich
5. ☐	cooker	e) Gabel	13. ☐	spoon	m) Ofen
6. ☐	shower	f) Tiefkühler	14. ☐	toilet	n) Waschbecken
7. ☐	oven	g) Kühlschrank	15. ☐	fridge	o) Messer
8. ☐	plate	h) Wohnung	16. ☐	knife	p) Regal

ÜBUNG 3:

Beschreiben Sie Ihre Wohnung! Wie viele Zimmer haben Sie, welche Farben haben Ihre Möbel? Verwenden Sie die Begriffe aus Übung 2 und bilden Sie Sätze wie ...

Rätselkärtchen

Welcher der Sätze ist grammatikalisch richtig?

He didn't reading a book. d

She didn't call him. e

Lösungswort für Lektion 8: _ _ _ _ _ _ _ _ _

Die Vokabelkärtchen gibt es auf **www.lernkrimi.de**

My flat/house has ______________ rooms:

____

In the living room, there are ______________________________

My favourite armchair is (colour) ______________________________

I bought this table in (year, place) ______________________________

____

____

____

____

____

2-17

I called Scotland Yard. I spoke to a crime scene investigation officer. London police were on the alert. An incident room was set up. I set off in the car to go to Elvira's house. I wanted to see Miss Paddington. I was worried. Suddenly, the phone rang. It was Victor. He was calling from Brighton.

"I have some bad news," he said. "You must come to Brighton immediately. Elvira has been kidnapped!"

2-18

ÜBUNG 1:

Hören Sie zu und setzen Sie die richtige Verbform ein!

At Brighton police station, a team of police officers (1. wait) ________________ for me. "The man in black (2. murder) ____________________ my colleague," I (3. say) __________. "He (4. attack) ______________________ my boss. He (5. set) ________________ my house on fire. Now I think he (6. kidnap) ______________________ a very good friend. This is personal. He must be stopped. Elvira's life (7. be) ____________ in danger."

ÜBUNG 2:

*Schreiben Sie das **Simple Past** und das **Past Participle** der folgenden Verben auf! Achten Sie auf Unregelmäßigkeiten!*

Infinitive	*Simple Past*	*Past Participle*
1. write	wrote	written
2. find	____________________	____________________
3. call	____________________	____________________
4. go	____________________	____________________
5. say	____________________	____________________
6. come	____________________	____________________
7. see	____________________	____________________
8. eat	____________________	____________________

9. be ____________________ ____________________

10. do ____________________ ____________________

Rätselkärtchen

Richtig ✓ oder falsch ×? ✓ ×

Somebody kidnapped Elvira. w u

Elvira kidnapped somebody. e i

ÜBUNG 3:

Setzen Sie die Verben in Klammern ins ***Present Perfect****!*

1. She's a writer. She (write) ***has written*** four books.
2. Hudson (go) ____________________ to Brighton.
3. The police are investigating. They (find) ____________________ a clue.
4. Brighton is nice. Elvira (be) ____________________ there twice.
5. Only two people (see) ____________________ the man in black.
6. Do you want another biscuit? – No, I (have) ____________________ five already!

GRAMMATIK

Das Present Perfect

Das **Present Perfect** wird mit ***have/has*** und dem **Past Participle** (Partizip II) gebildet. Das **Past Perfect** ist bei regelmäßigen Verben immer mit dem **Simple Past** identisch, bei unregelmäßigen aber nur manchmal:

call	*call**ed***	*call**ed***	(regelmäßig)
write	***wrote***	***written***	(unregelmäßig)

Das **Present Perfect** wird verwendet, wenn eine Handlung in der Vergangenheit begonnen hat und bis zum jetzigen Zeitpunkt anhält:

Hudson ***has gone*** *to Brighton.* (He is still there now.)

She ***has written*** *four books.* (She will probably write more in the future.)

Ebenso wird das **Present Perfect** benutzt, wenn etwas gerade geschehen ist, die genaue Zeit jedoch keine Rolle spielt:

The police ***have just found*** *a clue.* (A moment ago.)

Das **Simple Past** wird hingegen verwendet, wenn eine Handlung zu einem bestimmten Zeitpunkt in der Vergangenheit stattgefunden hat und abgeschlossen ist:

Hudson ***arrived*** *in Brighton at 4 p.m.*

2-19

"Have you found any witnesses, or any clues?" I asked.
"We have some witnesses," said Sergeant Christopher Hobden. "At around 8.50 a.m. this morning, some people saw a black car on Kingsway. They saw Miss Elliot talking to someone in the car. Then Miss Elliot got into the car."
"Did any of the people get the license plate number?" I asked.
"No," he said.
"That's a pity."
"Some of the officers have interviewed Victor Crawley. At 8.30 a.m. Miss Elliot went to the bakery."
"Did she buy anything?" I asked.
"Yes. She bought some bread, orange juice and milk."

ÜBUNG 1:

2-20

*Setzen Sie **any** oder **some** in die Lücken ein! Hören Sie danach die Sätze auf der CD und sprechen Sie nach!*

1. Did you buy __________ milk?
2. I don't have __________ money.
3. We have __________ soap. Don't buy __________.
4. I want __________ cheese and __________ tomatoes.
5. He doesn't want __________thing.
6. __________ people like shopping.

ÜBUNG 2:

***Simple Past** or **Present Perfect**? Setzen Sie die Begriffe mit der richtigen Verbform ein! Achten Sie dabei besonders auf die Zeitangaben!*

1. a) (the inspector/go) *Has the inspector gone to Brighton?*
   b) Yes, (he/go) ____________________ there yesterday.

2. a) (you/find) ________________________ any witnesses yet?

   b) Yes, (we/find) ________________________ some people who saw the car.

3. a) (you/see) ________________________ Elvira?

   b) Yes, (I/see) ________________________ her three days ago.

ÜBUNG 3:

Verbinden Sie die englischen Begriffe mit ihrer Übersetzung!

1. ☐	bread	a) Gemüse
2. ☐	chicken	b) Käse
3. ☐	cheese	c) Butter
4. ☐	beef	d) Eier
5. ☐	cake	e) Rindfleisch
6. ☐	vegetables	f) Kuchen
7. ☐	butter	g) Wasser
8. ☐	eggs	h) Brot
9. ☐	potatoes	i) Hühnchen
10. ☐	water	j) Kartoffeln

Rätselkärtchen

Did Elvira buy __________?

r something   t anything

Elvira bought __________ bread.

n some   p any

GRAMMATIK

Some und any

Sowohl ***some*** als auch ***any*** kann mit **einige/etwas** übersetzt werden. Im Englischen ist es wichtig, beide Wörter zu verwenden, auch wenn man im Deutschen ihre Entsprechung oft weglassen kann.

Some wird in positiven Sätzen gebraucht, ***any*** in negierten Sätzen und in Fragen:

I would like ***some*** *chocolate.*	Ich hätte gern **etwas** Schokolade.
Do you have ***any*** *chocolate?*	Hast du Schokolade?
No, ***I don't*** *have* ***any*** *chocolate.*	Nein, ich habe **keine** Schokolade.

! Bietet man jemandem etwas an, wird auch in der Frage ***some*** benutzt:
Would you like ***some*** *biscuits?*

Die gleichen Regeln gelten für ***somebody/anybody***, ***someone/anyone*** und ***something/anything***.

2-21

I went to Victor's holiday flat. It was in a beautiful 1930s building. It had a view of the sea. Victor opened the door.
"You can't find her, can you?" he said.
"Not yet," I said.
"This man in black is the perfect criminal, isn't he?" said Victor. "You can't catch him. And now he has kidnapped Elvira."
"We will find her," I said.
Just then my mobile rang.
It was an officer from Brighton police station, James Marter.
"We have some good news," he said. "We found a witness who saw the black car license plate! The black car was a Mercedes. It was a rental car."

ÜBUNG 1:

*Setzen Sie die passenden **Question Tags** ein!*

1. You have, ***haven't you?***
2. She has, ______________________________?
3. They didn't, ___________________________?
4. They did, _____________________________?
5. He can't, _____________________________?
6. It hasn't,______________________________?

Inspector Hudson empfiehlt:

Nutzen Sie jede Gelegenheit, um Englisch zu üben. Auch Wartezeiten beim Arzt, an der Bushaltestelle oder am Flughafen können Sie wahrnehmen, um zu buchstabieren, zu zählen oder Gegenstände zu benennen.

ÜBUNG 2:

***Who** or **which**? Setzen Sie das korrekte Relativpronomen ein!*

1. That's the car __________ was parked on the street!
2. That's the man __________ rented the car.

3. She's the woman __________ can help us.
4. Here's the shop __________ sells hats.
5. That's the criminal __________ stole the handbag!
6. Find the place __________ rents cars.

Rätselkärtchen

The man ________ kidnapped Elvira is the man in black.

[e] who [a] which

The car ________ he drove was black.

[z] who [s] which

GRAMMATIK

Question Tags

Eine der deutschen Sprache gänzlich unbekannte Eigenheit des Englischen ist die Verwendung von **Question Tags**. Man kann sie etwa mit **nicht wahr?/oder?** ins Deutsche übersetzen.
Die **Question Tags** werden an das Ende eines Satzes gehängt. Ist der Satz positiv, wird ein negativer **Question Tag** verwendet und andersherum.
Der **Question Tag** wird mit einem Hilfsverb (***be***, ***have***, ***can***) oder mit ***to do*** gebildet.

He is an inspector, ***isn't*** *he?*	*He isn't a thief,* ***is*** *he?*
Elvira has a red car, ***hasn't*** *she?*	*She hasn't got blond hair,* ***has*** *she?*
They can swim, ***can't*** *they?*	*They can't drive,* ***can*** *they?*
You drink tea, ***don't*** *you?*	*You don't like peanuts,* ***do*** *you?*

! Die verneinte Form von ***will*** ist ***won't***!
You ***will*** *find her,* ***won't*** *you?*

Das Relativpronomen

Relativpronomen ersetzen ein Substantiv. Im Englischen werden ***who*** oder ***that*** für eine Person verwendet, ***which*** oder ***that*** für Dinge:
The witness ***who/that*** *saw the car.*
I don't like films ***which/that*** *are very scary.*

Um über einen Ort zu sprechen, wird ***where*** verwendet:
That's the flat ***where*** *Victor lives.*

9.4 FOOD AND DRINK

2-22

At the car rental agency I spoke to the receptionist. She was very helpful. A man called Ian Michael Moriarty had rented the Mercedes that morning. He was tall and thin. He wore a black coat and hat, and black sunglasses. He had long red hair.

"His hair was funny," said the receptionist. "It looked like a wig!"

I got back to the station. I went into the incident room. Some officers were there. They were looking on computers and making telephone calls. I told them about the rental car.

"Let's look at CCTV," I said. "There might be CCTV cameras on Kingsway, and at the car rental agency, too."

ÜBUNG 1:

Lesen Sie die Sätze und schreiben Sie auf, in welcher Zeitform sie stehen!
(Simple Past, Present Continuous, Future, Past Continuous, Present Simple, Present Perfect)

1. They were making telephone calls. ____________________
2. I went into the incident room. ____________________
3. They have found a witness. ____________________
4. He's a police officer. ____________________
5. Hudson will catch the kidnapper. ____________________
6. I'm trying to find a witness. ____________________

ÜBUNG 2:

Verbinden Sie die Adjektive mit dem passenden Substantiv!

1. ☐ building	a) lovely, beautiful, rainy
2. ☐ car	b) good, bad, interesting
3. ☐ woman	c) tall, beautiful, modern
4. ☐ news	d) black, fast, big
5. ☐ day	e) tall, good-looking, intelligent

Rätselkärtchen

Richtig ✓ oder falsch ×? ✓ ×

Hudson spoke to the hat seller. r s

2-23

ÜBUNG 3:

Setzen Sie die fehlenden Begriffe ein und schreiben Sie auf, um wen es sich handelt! Hören Sie anschließend die CD an und überprüfen Sie die Antworten!
(solves, short, insurance, grey (2x), big, hat, tall, coat, Scotland Yard, moustache, red, thin, black, wears, crime, watching, commits)

1. She's ______________ and fat. She's got ______________ hair. She's a housekeeper. She likes ____________________ crime movies.
It's _______________________

2. He's got dark hair and he _____________________ a brown ______________ and hat. He works at __________________________. He _________________ crime.
It's ________________________

3. He's 53 years old. He's got _______________ hair and a __________________. He's rich and lives in a ________________ house.
It's ________________________

4. She's got long ________________ hair. She's thin and _____________. She works at an _______________________ company and she likes to solve ______________.
It's _________________________

5. He's tall and _________________. He wears a _______________ coat and ____________. Sometimes he wears a wig. He _________________ crime.
WHO IS IT?

GRAMMATIK

Might und may

Might und **may** sind Hilfsverben und werden verwendet, um eine Wahrscheinlichkeit auszudrücken. Sie sind in der Regel austauschbar:

*He **might/may** be the man in black.* Er ist vielleicht der Mann in Schwarz.

In Fragesätzen stellt **may/might** die Bitte um eine Erlaubnis dar.

***May/might** I help you?* Darf/dürfte ich Ihnen behilflich sein?

Present Perfect und Simple Past

Es ist wichtig, genau zwischen dem **Present Perfect** und dem **Simple Past** zu unterscheiden, da sich sonst leicht Missverständnisse ergeben können. Beachten Sie, dass man das **Present Perfect** im Deutschen manchmal sogar mit dem Präsens übersetzt!

*I've **lived** in London for four years.* Ich **wohne** seit vier Jahren in London.
*I **lived** in London for four years.* Ich **wohnte** vier Jahre lang in London.

*I **moved** to London four years ago.* Ich **bin** vor vier Jahren nach London **gezogen**.
In diesem Satz steht die Handlung des (abgeschlossenen) Umzugs im Vordergrund, auch wenn das Wohnen noch andauert.

– ***Have** you **seen** him lately?* – Hast du ihn in letzter Zeit gesehen?
– *I **saw** him yesterday.* – Ich habe ihn gestern gesehen (abgeschlossene Handlung).

ÜBUNG 1:

*Verbinden Sie die Sätze mit dem passenden **Question Tag**!*

1. ☐ He is the perfect criminal,
2. ☐ You can't catch him,
3. ☐ You don't know Elvira,
4. ☐ You've been to Brighton,

a) haven't you?
b) do you?
c) can you?
d) isn't he?

Tier oder Fleisch?

Im Gegensatz zum Deutschen wird im Englischen in einigen Fällen ein Unterschied gemacht, ob ein Tier lebendig ist oder als Stück Fleisch auf dem Teller liegt:

Tier	**Fleisch**	
cow	*beef*	Rind
pig	*pork*	Schwein
calf	*veal*	Kalb

aber:

Tier/Fleisch	
chicken	Huhn
lamb	Lamm
turkey	Pute/Truthahn
fish	Fisch

ÜBUNG 2:

Lesen Sie den Text und Übung 1 auf Seite 96 noch einmal durch und setzen Sie die fehlenden Partikel ein!

1. The incident room was set ________.
2. He set ________ in the police car.
3. My house was set ________ fire!

Solve the mystery of the man in black! Who is it?

Die Antwort liegt in den Lösungswörtern der Rätselkärtchen. Finden Sie die gesuchten Buchstaben und bringen Sie sie in die richtige Reihenfolge!

Rätselkärtchen

Unit 1
Das Lösungswort heißt:
_ _ _ _ _ _ _ _ _ _

Take the fifth letter: _

Rätselkärtchen

Unit 2
Das Lösungswort heißt:
_ _ _ _ _ _ _ _ _ _

Take the last letter: _

Rätselkärtchen

Unit 3
Das Lösungswort heißt: _ _ _ _ _ _ _ _ _ _

Take the fourth and the sixth letter: _ , _

Rätselkärtchen

Unit 4
Das Lösungswort heißt:
_ _ _ _ _ _ _ _ _ _ _

Take the second letter: _

Rätselkärtchen

Unit 5
Das Lösungswort heißt:
_ _ _ _ _ _ _ _ _

Take the fourth letter: _

Rätselkärtchen

Unit 6
Das Lösungswort heißt:
_ _ _ _ _ _ _ _ _ _

Take the fourth and the seventh letter: _ , _

Rätselkärtchen

Unit 7
Das Lösungswort heißt: _ _ _ _ _ _ _ _ _ _ _

Take the third letter of the first word and the fourth letter of the second word: _ , _

Rätselkärtchen

Unit 8
Das Lösungswort heißt:
_ _ _ _ _ _ _ _ _ _

Take the third and the last letter: _ , _

Rätselkärtchen

Unit 9
Das Lösungswort heißt:
_ _ _ _ _ _ _ _

Take the first letter: _

Lösung

Now mix the letters and you have solved the mystery!

The man in black is _ _ _ _ _ _ _ _ _ _ _ _ _ _ _ !

2-24

That evening I went back to my hotel. There was a letter waiting for me at reception.

> The great Inspector Hudson has failed. He can't solve every crime. You will never catch the man in black.

I called Miss Paddington.
"We haven't found Elvira yet," I said. "But we have some clues."
I told Miss Paddington about the car and Ian Michael Moriarty.
"What a funny name," she said.
"It's a false name," I said. "We have looked for him."
"Yes, but it's funny because Ian Michael Moriarty becomes IM Moriarty. I'm Moriarty. Do you know who that is?"
"No," I said.
"Moriarty was Sherlock Holmes's nemesis," she said.

ÜBUNG 1:

Finden Sie das passende Gegenteil und verbinden Sie!

1. ☐ false	a) slow
2. ☐ buy	b) short
3. ☐ long	c) true
4. ☐ interesting	d) bad
5. ☐ fast	e) sell
6. ☐ good	f) boring

Rätselkärtchen

Edinburgh is an ________ city.
h exciting   o excitingly

Please be ________!
a careful   u carefully

ÜBUNG 2:

Wandeln Sie die Adjektive in Adverbien um!

1. slow — *slowly*
2. loud — ________
3. quiet — ________
4. careful — ________
5. bad — ________
6. sudden — ________

ÜBUNG 3:

Setzen Sie die Adverbien aus Übung 2 in die Lücken ein!

1. He shouted at me ________________.
2. Please speak ________________. I can't understand you.
3. Sir Reginald was ________________ hurt.
4. ________________ the phone rang. I was surprised.
5. I went into the room ________________ because the baby was asleep.
6. Please think ________________ before you answer this question.

GRAMMATIK

Adverbien

Während Adjektive ein Substantiv näher beschreiben, bestimmen Adverbien das Verb genauer. Im Englischen werden die Adverbien gebildet, indem **-ly** an das Adjektiv angehängt wird:

*He is **slow**.*	Er ist langsam.
*She **speaks slowly**.*	Sie redet langsam.

Endet das Adjektiv auf **-e**, fällt dieses **-e** weg und das **-ly** wird an den Wortstamm gehängt:

*The murderer is a **terrible** man.*	Der Mörder ist ein schrecklicher Mann.
*He **smells terribly**.*	Er riecht schrecklich.

Im Gegensatz zum Deutschen unterscheiden sich im Englischen Adverb und Adjektiv meist voneinander.

Es gibt jedoch auch im Englischen Ausnahmen, bei denen sich Adjektiv und Adverb nicht voneinander unterscheiden, z. B.:

*He is **fast**.*	Er ist schnell.
*He **drives fast**.*	Er fährt schnell.

! Eine weitere Ausnahme bildet ***good***, dessen Adverb in der Regel ***well*** heißt.

2-25

At 10.30 p.m. the Brighton police team and I went to Victor's holiday flat. We knocked on the door. Victor answered.

"Inspector," he said. "Do you have any information about Elvira?"

"Yes," I replied. "You are the man in black, Victor. I am arresting you for theft, arson, assault, murder and kidnapping."

"What?" said Victor. "This is a joke! You can't prove it!"

"You started with small crimes. Then the crimes got bigger. They got worse. You threw the burning bottle through the window. A moment later you called my mobile and left a message. But it was a pre-recorded message. You weren't in your car."

ÜBUNG 1:

Setzen Sie die richtigen Positiv-, Komparativ- und Superlativformen in die Lücken ein!
(best, younger, biggest, worse, earlier, youngest, most intelligent, old, nicest, beautiful, bigger, more beautiful, nice, intelligent, older)

Positiv	*Komparativ*	*Superlativ*
1. big	______	______
2. bad	______	worst
3. ______	more intelligent	______
4. good	better	______
5. ______	______	oldest
6. ______	nicer	______
7. young	______	______
8. ______	______	most beautiful
9. early	______	earliest

ÜBUNG 2:

Übersetzen Sie die Begriffe in Klammern!

"Come on, Inspector," says Miss Paddington. "I (1. muss) ______ lose weight and you're out of shape, too. Let's go swimming!"

Rätselkärtchen

Hudson is ______ than Miss Paddington.

n taller   s more tall

Elvira is ______ than Victor.

t beautifuller   d more beautiful

"No, Miss Paddington, I'm (2. zu müde) ______________________."

"But remember! The man in black was (3. zu schnell) _________________ for you. Let's go jogging!"

"No, he wasn't too fast. There were (4. zu viele) _________________ people."

"Let's go on a bike tour then. We could go to Brighton!"

"Are you mad? That's 50 miles! No, I stay (5. zu Hause) ______________________."

GRAMMATIK

Der Komparativ

Es gibt zwei Möglichkeiten, den regelmäßigen Komparativ (Vergleichsform) im Englischen zu bilden. Hat das Adjektiv ein oder zwei Silben, wird ein ***-er*** angehängt. Endet das Adjektiv auf ***-y***, wird dieses durch ein ***-i-*** ersetzt:

slow	*slow**er***	*pretty*	*prett**ier***

Adjektiven mit mehr als zwei Silben wird ein ***more*** vorangestellt, ohne dass das Adjektiv selbst sich verändert:

beautiful	***more** beautiful*

Der Superlativ

Hier gelten die gleichen Regeln wie beim Komparativ. An Adjektive mit ein oder zwei Silben wird ein ***-est*** angehängt. Die Endung ***-y*** wird durch ein ***-i-*** ersetzt.

slow	*slower*	*slow**est***
pretty	*prettier*	*prett**iest***

Adjektiven mit mehr als zwei Silben wird ein ***most*** vorangestellt, ohne dass das Adjektiv selbst sich verändert:

beautiful	*more beautiful*	***most** beautiful*

Mehr zum Vergleich im Grammatikteil auf S. 114 und 133–134.

2-26

"You murdered Constable Watson because she was helping the investigation. Then you brought Elvira to Brighton. Elvira left the flat to buy bread. You left the flat a moment later. You ran to the rented Mercedes. You drove to the bakery, then told Elvira to get into the car. Later you gave her drugs and brought her back to the flat."

I went into the bedroom. I opened the wardrobe door. Elvira was lying in the wardrobe. She was tied up. I called the other officers to help her.

Then I put handcuffs on Victor.

"You said the man in black was the perfect criminal," I told him. "You created crimes to trick me. But you don't know Miss Paddington! When she told me about IM Moriarty, I knew it was you."

2-27

ÜBUNG 1:

Setzen Sie die fehlenden Begriffe ein! Hören Sie danach die Sätze auf der CD und sprechen Sie nach!

(through, any, turned, some, threw, left, broke)

1. Last night he ______________ the bottle and ______________ the glass.
2. He looked ________________ the window.
3. At the end of the street I ______________ left.
4. After the interview I ______________.
5. The police found ______________ witnesses.
6. The police didn't find ______________ clues.

ÜBUNG 2:

Schreiben Sie den ersten Absatz des Texts ins ***Past Perfect*** *(Vorvergangenheit) um!*

"You had murdered Constable Watson because she had been helping the investigation. Then you had brought Elvira to Brighton. ____

____

Rätselkärtchen

Before he ____________ to Brighton, ...

c went o had gone

... the criminal __________ Miss Paddinton's handbag.

r stole u had stolen

ÜBUNG 3:

Verbinden Sie die Ausdrücke mit ihrer Übersetzung!

1. ☐ jogging	a) schwimmen
2. ☐ bike tour	b) Klettern
3. ☐ hiking	c) Fußball spielen
4. ☐ to swim	d) Jogging
5. ☐ to run	e) Tennis spielen
6. ☐ rock climbing	f) Fahrradtour
7. ☐ to play football	g) Wandern
8. ☐ to play tennis	h) laufen

GRAMMATIK

Das Past Perfect

Mit dem **Past Perfect** werden Ereignisse beschrieben, die vor einem bestimmten Zeitpunkt in der Vergangenheit stattgefunden haben. Regelmäßige Verben bilden das **Past Perfect** mit ***had*** + **Partizip Perfekt**, das der Form des **Simple Past** entspricht:

*Hudson **had stayed** in Edinburgh **before** he **came** back to London.*

Das **Partizip Perfekt** der unregelmäßigen Verben muss gelernt werden. Eine Liste der unregelmäßigen Verben finden Sie auf den Seiten 138–140.

*The criminal **had set** Hudson's house on fire **before** he **kidnapped** Elvira.*

(!) Das **Partizip Perfekt** von ***to be*** ist ***been***!

2-28

A few nights later Elvira and I went into a Brighton pub. All the officers who had worked with us were there, too.
"I'm buying drinks for everybody!" I said. The officers cheered.
"I'm glad you're safe," I told Elvira.
"Thanks for finding me, James," she said. "Victor Crawley was wrong. Even a criminal mastermind can't stop Inspector Hudson."

ÜBUNG 1:

*Setzen Sie das Verb in Klammern in die richtige Zeitform! Benutzen Sie **going to**!*

1. a) What are you *going to do* tonight, Inspector?
   b) I'm (go) ________________ to the pub with the Brighton police officers.

2. a) What are you (do) ________________ tonight, Elvira?
   b) I'm (have) ________________ a drink with my friend James.

3. a) What are you (do) ________________ tomorrow, Sir Reginald?
   b) I'm (leave) ________________ hospital and go home.

4. a) What are you (do) ________________ today, Miss Paddington?
   b) I'm (relax) ________________ and watch a crime film.

ÜBUNG 2:

*Und was werden Sie tun? Beantworten Sie die Fragen mit **going to** + Verb mit ihren eigenen Worten!*

1. Tonight? ____

____

2. Tomorrow morning? ______________________________

3. Tomorrow night? ______________________________

4. On Sunday? ______________________________

5. Next week? ______________________________

6. In the summer? ______________________________

Rätselkärtchen

Richtig ✓ oder falsch ×?

	✓	×
Hudson will go to prison.	n	f
Elvira will marry Victor.	w	f

GRAMMATIK

Das Futur

Es gibt zwei Arten, die Zukunft auszudrücken: ***will*** oder ***going to*** + **Infinitiv**.
Going to wird verwendet, wenn es um die eigenen Pläne geht, die bereits feststehen:
*I'**m going to read** a detective story tonight.*

Will ist meist mit ***going to*** austauschbar:
*Victor **will go** to prison.*
*Victor **is going to go** to prison.*

Oft steht ***will*** jedoch bei einem weniger konkreten Ereignis in der Zukunft:
*Sir Reginald **will** die.* (Eines Tages wird er sterben.)
*Sir Reginald **is going to** die.* (Er wird bald sterben.)

Der Vergleich

Wenn zwei Dinge im Vergleich ebenbürtig abschneiden, wird ***as ... as*** benutzt:

Elvira's car is ***as red as*** *her hair.* Elviras Auto ist **so rot wie** ihre Haare.

Schneiden die Dinge im Vergleich unterschiedlich ab, wird der **Komparativ +** ***than*** benutzt:

Inspector Hudson's car is ***bigger than*** *Elvira's car.* Das Auto von Inspector Hudson ist **größer als** Elviras Auto.

! Wie im Deutschen gibt es einige Adjektive, die den Komparativ und den Superlativ unregelmäßig bilden, z. B.:

good	***better***	***best***
bad	***worse***	***worst***

Bei kurzen Adjektiven mit kurzem Vokal wird der Endkonsonant verdoppelt:

big	*bigger*	*biggest*
fat	*fatter*	*fattest*

ÜBUNG 1:

Setzen Sie das passende Adjektiv mit ***as ... as*** *ein!*
(interesting, big, good, long, slow)

1. My friend runs slowly. She's ______________________ me.
2. Your English is good. It's ______________________ mine.
3. His football is ______________________ mine.
4. Tennis is ______________________ football.
5. The distance London – Brighton is ______________________ London – Cambridge.

ÜBUNG 2:

Setzen Sie das Adjektiv in Klammern in den Komparativ!

1. Elvira is (fit)_________________ than Miss Paddington.
2. Inspector Hudson is (lazy) ___________________ than Miss Paddington.
3. Sir Reginald is (old) _______________________ than Elvira.
4. Today's weather is (bad) _______________________ than yesterday's weather.
5. Victor thinks he is (intelligent) ________________________ than Inspector Hudson.

ÜBUNG 3:

Setzen Sie das Adjektiv in Klammern in den Superlativ!

1. Inspector Hudson is the (smart) ________________________ policeman on earth.
2. Elvira is the (pretty) ________________________________ woman in London.
3. How much?! This is the (expensive) ______________________________ hotel I've ever slept in!
4. This cake is the (delicious) _____________________________ I've ever tasted.
5. The man in black is the (bad) ______________________ criminal I've ever met!

Rätselkärtchen

Welcher der Sätze ist grammatikalisch richtig?

He's going to go on holiday next week. [s]

She been on holiday last week. [d]

Lösungswort für Lektion 10: _ _ _ _ _ _ _ _ _ _

Die Vokabelkärtchen gibt es auf **www.lernkrimi.de**

Das Past Perfect

Wie im Deutschen steht das **Past Perfect** für die sogenannte Vorvergangenheit, d.h. ein Ereignis hat vor einem bestimmten Zeitpunkt in der Vergangenheit stattgefunden:

*He **had seen** the film several times **before** he **bought** the dvd.*

Er **hatte** den Film mehrfach **gesehen** **bevor** er die DVD **kaufte**.

ÜBUNG 4:

Sind die folgenden Aussagen korrekt? Markieren Sie mit richtig ✓ oder falsch ×!

1. The man in black had kidnapped Elvira before he killed her. ☐
2. Inspector Hudson had bought the train tickets before he went to Edinburgh. ☐
3. Elvira had been together with Victor before he kidnapped her. ☐
4. Miss Paddington had stolen wallets before she became a housekeeper. ☐
5. Constable Watson had helped the investigation before she was murdered. ☐
6. Victor Crawley is going to stay in prison for a long time. ☐
7. Hudson and Elvira will get married. ☐
8. Sir Reginald is going to leave the hospital. ☐

WIEDERHOLUNG 3

Gratulation, Sie haben nun alle Lektionen geschafft und nebenbei auch noch einen Verbrecher entlarvt! Auf den folgenden Seiten können Sie das Gelernte nochmals vertiefen, bevor Sie mit dem Abschlusstest Ihre Englischkenntnisse überprüfen.

ÜBUNG 1:

*Bilden Sie Fragen mit **did** und den Begriffen in Klammern!*

1. (Hudson/stay/Edinburgh) ______________________________________?
2. (they/find/clue) ______________________________________?
3. (you/go/doctor's) ______________________________________?

ÜBUNG 2:

*Setzen Sie **for**, **ago**, oder **at** in die Lücken ein!*

1. When did you go to London? Two weeks __________.
2. What time did he ring? __________11.45 a.m.
3. How long were you at the hospital? __________ four hours.
4. How long did you work for Scotland Yard? __________ twelve years.
5. When did you see Elvira? Thirty minutes __________.

ÜBUNG 3:

*Unterstreichen Sie die Sätze im **Past Continuous**!*

1. The glass broke/The glass was breaking.
2. I was reading a crime story/I am reading a crime story.
3. They are going on holiday/They were going on holiday.
4. Hudson was waiting downstairs/Hudson waits downstairs.

ÜBUNG 4:

*Setzen Sie **listen** oder **hear** in die Lücken ein!*

1. Can you __________ the phone ringing?
2. __________! What's that sound?
3. __________ to me when I'm talking. It's important!
4. I can't __________ you. Please speak louder.

ÜBUNG 5:

*Was muss getan werden? Bilden Sie Sätze mit **to have to**!*

1. Tomorrow/I/read this crime story.

____

2. Tonight/you/have a shower.

____

3. Next week/we/buy new clothes.

____

4. Tomorrow morning/he/go to work.

____

5. At 3.30/they/catch the train.

____

6. Later/she/feed the dog.

____

ÜBUNG 6:

*Verneinen Sie die Sätze mit **didn't/wasn't**!*

1. The inspector bought a new coat. *The inspector didn't buy a new coat.*
2. We found a clue. ______________________
3. I was drinking coffee. ______________________
4. They went to Brighton. ______________________
5. She came to the party. ______________________
6. Sir Reginald got hurt. ______________________

ÜBUNG 7:

***Present Perfect** oder **Simple Past** ? Wählen Sie die richtige Zeitform!*

1. Inspector Hudson __________ at Scotland Yard for twelve years.

a) ☐ worked b) ☐ has worked

2. I like films. I __________ to the cinema ten times this year.

a) ☐ have been b) ☐ was

3. She __________ in Brighton for three years. Now she lives in London.
a) ☐ has lived b) ☐ lived

4. Would you like more coffee? – No, thanks. I __________ two cups already!
a) ☐ had b) ☐ have had

ÜBUNG 8:

*Setzen Sie **some** oder **any** in die Lücken ein!*

1. Would you like __________ cake?
2. Please buy __________ orange juice and __________ bread.
3. I don't have __________thing to eat!
4. Don't buy __________ eggs. We have __________.
5. Have the police found __________ clues yet?

ÜBUNG 9:

Beschreiben Sie die Personen!

1. Inspector Hudson is ____
____
____

2. Elvira Elliot is ____
____
____

3. Miss Paddington is ____
____
____

ÜBUNG 10:

Adjektiv oder Adverb? Unterstreichen Sie die richtige Variante!

1. She shouted loudly/loud.
2. Please be carefully/careful!
3. English people are very polite/politely.
4. He speaks English well/good.
5. Elvira drives very fastly/fast.

ÜBUNG 11:

Komparativ oder Superlativ? Bilden Sie die richtige Vergleichsform aus dem Adjektiv in Klammern!

1. Your car is (big) _______________ than my car.
2. That's the (red) _______________ strawberry I've ever seen.
3. Ice cream is the (delicious) _______________ food in the world.
4. My day was (bad) _______________ than your day.
5. Those shoes are (expensive) _______________ than these shoes.

ÜBUNG 12:

Verwandeln Sie die Sätze mit ***will*** *oder* ***going to*** *und den Verben in Klammern!*

1. (go) I think I _______________ to London next year.
2. (meet) Hudson is _______________ the police officers in a pub tonight.
3. (have) Coffee or tea? I _______________ coffee, please.
4. (do) What are you _______________ tonight?

Jetzt können Sie ...

- Ihre Körperteile benennen.
- sagen, wo Sie Schmerzen haben.
- Schmerzen beschreiben.
- Fragen in der Vergangenheitsform stellen.
- Präpositionen verwenden.
- Aussagen über die Zukunft machen.
- mitteilen, dass Sie ebenfalls etwas möchten.
- sich differenziert in den verschiedenen Vergangenheitsformen ausdrücken.
- Zeiträume angeben.
- Ihre Meinung ausdrücken.
- Ihre Pläne mitteilen.
- Gebote und Verbote formulieren.
- Vergleiche ziehen.
- Aussagen über Essen machen.
- Fragen mit *Question Tags* stellen.
- Substantive durch Relativpronomen ersetzen.
- Menschen beschreiben.
- die Umstände einer Handlung beschreiben.
- über Sport sprechen.

UND Kriminalfälle lösen!

ÜBUNG 1:

Bringen Sie die Wochentage in die richtige Reihenfolge!

☐ Tuesday ☐ Friday ☐ Sunday ☐ Saturday
☐ Monday ☐ Thursday ☐ Wednesday

ÜBUNG 2:

Setzen Sie die korrekten Possessivpronomen ein!

1. Hudson is in __________ office. (he)
2. Sir Reginald is __________ boss. (me)
3. She can't find __________ handbag. (she)
4. Please come to __________ party! (we)
5. That's __________ house. (they)
6. What is __________ phone number? (he)

ÜBUNG 3:

Setzen Sie in die Lücken die passenden Fragewörter ein!

1. __________ kidnapped Elvira? – The man in black.
2. __________ did Hudson and Miss Paddington go on holiday? – Edinburgh.
3. __________ did Elvira and Hudson meet? – At 3.30.
4. __________ did they eat at the café? – Chocolate cake.
5. __________ did Hudson go to his office? – Because he had to work.

ÜBUNG 4:

Schauen Sie sich die Uhren an und schreiben Sie die Uhrzeiten auf!

1.  ______________________
2.  ______________________
3.  ______________________
4.  ______________________
5.  ______________________
6.  ______________________

7.  ____________________

8.  ____________________

9.  ____________________

10.  ____________________

ÜBUNG 5:

*Bilden Sie Sätze im **Present Continuous**!*

1. (I/work) ____________________________

2. (We/talk) ____________________________

4. (He/eat and drink) ____________________________

5. (She/sit/in a café) ____________________________

6. (They/go/on holiday) ____________________________

ÜBUNG 6:

Verbinden Sie die Wörter mit ihrer Übersetzung!

1. ☐ Don't worry.	a) Vorsicht!
2. ☐ Help!	b) Bis später.
3. ☐ No Problem.	c) Vielleicht.
4. ☐ Maybe.	d) Keine Sorge.
5. ☐ See you later.	e) Hilfe!
6. ☐ Careful!	f) Kein Problem.

ÜBUNG 7:

Setzen Sie die Verben in die 3. Person Singular (he/she/it). Achten Sie dabei besonders auf die Endungen, die nicht regelmäßig gebildet werden!

1. do ______________	6. play ______________
2. go ______________	7. hear ______________
3. see ______________	8. push ______________
4. kiss ______________	9. say ______________
5. leave ______________	10. watch ______________

ÜBUNG 8:

*Ordnen Sie die Häufigkeitsadverben von **nie** bis **immer**!*

☐ always ☐ never ☐ often ☐ sometimes ☐ seldom

ÜBUNG 9:

*Geben Sie die Vergangenheitsform (**Simple Past**) der folgenden Verben an!*

1. is ____________
2. say ____________
3. want ____________
4. do ____________
5. go ____________
6. pay ____________
7. are ____________
8. see ____________
9. come ____________

ÜBUNG 10:

Geben Sie die Pluralform an!

1. story ________________
2. sandwich ________________
3. policeman ________________
4. burglary ________________
5. information ________________
6. message ________________
7. woman ________________
8. thief ________________
9. gallery ________________
10. taxi ________________

ÜBUNG 11:

Wie lautet die richtige Übersetzung der folgenden Wörter?

1. sore ________________
2. stomach ________________
3. cough ________________
4. throat ________________
5. headache ________________
6. knee ________________

ÜBUNG 12:

*Schreiben Sie die folgenden Sätze im **Past Continuous**. Benutzen Sie **was** oder **were**!*

1. We are talking. ____

2. I am waiting. ______________________

3. Elvira is meeting me. ______________________

4. They are going on holiday. ______________________

5. He is reading a book. ______________________

ÜBUNG 13:

Unterstreichen Sie die richtige Variante!

1. Hudson is working/works for Scotland Yard.
2. The criminal breaked/broke the window.
3. Tonight I'm going to have/I have a dinner party.
4. I think I have/I'll have coffee, please.
5. At the moment we learn/are learning English.

ÜBUNG 14:

Übersetzen Sie!

1. Turn right ______________________
2. At the lights ______________________
3. Go along Queen Street ______________________
4. On the left ______________________
5. At the end of the street ______________________
6. Past the Scott Monument ______________________
7. Turn right ______________________
8. Take the second left ______________________

ÜBUNG 15:

Ergänzen Sie die fehlenden Verbformen!

Infinitve	*Simple Past*	*Past Participle*
1. *write*	____________	____________
2. ____________	*found*	____________

3. *go*	__________	__________
4. __________	*ate*	__________
5. __________	__________	*seen*
6. *be*	__________	*been*
7. __________	*talked*	__________

ÜBUNG 16:

Komparativ oder Superlativ? Wählen Sie die passende Steigerungsform!

1. My friend is 28. I am 30. I am ______________ than her.
2. That wine is my favourite. It's the ______________ wine I've ever drunk.
3. My friends are 33. I am 38. I am the ______________.
4. Roses are beautiful. They're ________________________ than lilies.
5. They speak English well, but my English is the ______________.
6. Lilies are beautiful. They're the ________________________ flowers in the world.
7. I don't like this wine. I think it's the ______________ wine I've ever drunk.

4\. They speak English well, but my English is ______________ than theirs.

ÜBUNG 17:

Verbinden Sie die Sätze mit der richtigen Zeitform!

1. ☐ I think I'll finish work early today.	a) Future with "going to"
2. ☐ She works for an insurance company.	b) Past Simple
3. ☐ We are drinking coffee and eating cake.	c) Present Perfect
4. ☐ Tonight I'm going to meet the police officers.	d) Past Continuous
5. ☐ He was waiting for me at the Hospital.	e) Present Simple
6. ☐ Victor attacked Sir Reginald.	f) Future
7. ☐ She has written four books.	g) Present Continuous

Unit 1

1.1 Übung 1: 1. d 2. f 3. e 4. b 5. a 6. c
Übung 4: 1. Monday 2. Tuesday 3. Wednesday 4. Thursday 5. Friday 6. Saturday 7. Sunday
1.2 Übung 1: 1. is 2. are 3. is 4. have 5. read
Übung 2: 1. ich esse 2. sie trinken 3. er kann 4. sie steigt aus 5. wir hören 6. du spielst/ihr spielt/Sie spielen 7. tragen 8. groß 9. wunderbar 10. glücklich 11. Kleid 12. schwarz
Übung 3: 1. name 2. work 3. I am 4. big 5. to be 6. dress
1.3 Übung 1: 1. Fine 2. How are 3. This is 4. this is 5. Nice
Übung 2: 1. It's 2. He's 3. She's 4. I'm 5. It's
Übung 3: 3, 2, 5, 6, 1, 7, 4
Übung 4: 1. we're 2. it's 3. he's 4. you're 5. they're 6. she's 7. I'm 8. here's
1.4 Übung 1: 1. solve 2. gets 3. He's 4. glass 5. card 6. help 7. Thanks
Übung 2: 1. d 2. a 3. e 4. f 5. c 6. b
Übung 3: 1. I'm fine, thanks. 2. Yes, I do. 3. I'm a policeman.

Grammatik

Übung 1: 1. is 2. drinks 3. is 4. wears 5. look 6. says 7. go 8. brings 9. likes
Übung 2: 1. an 2. a 3. a 4. an 5. a
Übung 4: 1. their 2. your 3. our 4. his 5. her 6. my

Unit 2

2.1 Übung 1: When 2. afternoon 3. nice 4. breakfast 5. later
Übung 2: 1. Er ruft Elvira an. 2. Elvira frühstückt mit Victor. 3. Sie verabreden sich in einem Café in der Castle Street.
Übung 3: 1. d 2. e 3. a 4. b 5. c
Übung 4: 1. When 2. Where 3. What
Übung 5: 7, 5, 4, 1, 6, 3, 2
2.2 Übung 1: 1. says 2. asks 3. who 4. answer 5. he 6. is 7. caller 8. thinks
Übung 2: 1. that 2. this 3. This 4. those 5. These
Übung 3: 1. a 2. b 3. a 4. a 5. b
2.3 Übung 1: 1. Who was the caller? 2. Was it a man or a woman? 3. What did he say? 4. Don't you think so?
Übung 2: 1. did 2. was 3. were
Übung 4: 1. three 2. ten 3. six 4. eight 5. twelve
2.4 Übung 1: 1. Sind Sie da? 2. Sie sind in Gefahr. 3. Nein, bin ich nicht. 4. Kommen Sie nach Hause. 5. Ich bin spät dran. 6. Machen Sie sich keine Sorgen.
Übung 2: 1. Where are you going? 2. Who is calling? 3. What do you do? 4. When shall we meet? 5. Why is he in danger? 6. How are you?
Übung 3: 1. b 2. a 3. a 4. a
Übung 4: 1. Come home! 2. Go to Scotland Yard! 3. Don't worry! 4. Be careful!

Grammatik

Übung 1: 1. How 2. Who 3. Where 4. What 5. Where
Übung 2: good, lovely, hot, nice, quiet, strange, red, red, nice, wonderful
Übung 3: 1. No, she has no housekeeper. 2. No, there is no reply when Hudson answers the phone. 3. No, there was no strange phone call. 4. No, I have no book.
Übung 4: 1. Victor was intelligent. 2. Who was the caller? 3. Is it a man or a woman? 4. There were two letters. 5. What did you write?

Unit 3

3.1 Übung 1: 1. What 2. I'd like 3. with 4. Anything 5. How 6. please
Übung 2: 1. She is waiting. 2. I am drinking. 3. They are talking. 4. We are meeting. 5. He is calling. 6. We are sitting in a café. 7. She is eating a muffin.

3.2 Übung 1: 1. e 2. f 3. h 4. g 5. b 6. d 7. a 8. c
Übung 2: 1. It's ten past four. 2. It's a quarter past seven. 3. It's half past eleven. 4. It's twenty to two. 5. It's a quarter to eight. 6. It's five to three. 7. It's half past eight. 8. It's eleven o'clock. 9. It's a quarter past five. 10. It's a quarter to one.
Übung 3: 1. coffee cup 2. chocolate cake 3. sugar 4. chocolate 5. blueberry muffin 6. blueberries

3.3 Übung 1: Everybody 2. Nobody 3. Somebody 4. Nobody 5. Everybody 6. Somebody
Übung 2: 1. I'm going. 2. She's driving. 3. We're looking. 4. He's eating. 5. They're shouting. 6. We're meeting. 7. I'm stealing. 8. You're standing up.
Übung 3: 1. Three twenty-seven. 2. Nine forty-three. 3. Eleven twenty-six. 4. Four fifteen. 5. Twelve eighteen. 6. Six thirty. 7. One thirty-nine. 8. Seven fifty-five.
Übung 4: 1. It's half past four. 2. It's five twenty. 3. It's midnight. 4. It's a quarter to two. 5. It's seven thirty-two. 6. It's six o'clock.

3.4 Übung 1: 1. Shall 2. Wednesday 3. go 4. Saturday 5. shopping 6. Sunday 7. I can't 8. going 9. loud
Übung 2: 1. No, they can't. 2. Yes, they can. 3. No, they can't. 4. No, they can't. 5. Yes, they can.
Übung 3: 1. No, it isn't. 2. No, it isn't. 3. Yes, it is.

Grammatik
Übung 1: 1. a 2. a 3. b 4. a 5. b 6. b
Übung 2: 1. Inspector Hudson gets strange phone calls. 2. He is meeting Elvira at a café. 3. Victor wants to help the inspector solve crimes. 4. Every week I meet Elvira for coffee. 5. Somebody is stealing wallets. 6. We need to get everybody's names and addresses.
Übung 3: 1. steal 2. help 3. criminal 4. enemy 5. careful Lösung: thief
Übung 4: 1. read, red, car 2. like, loud, concert 3. shout, nice, wallet 4. see, quiet, address 5. drive, good, thief

Wiederholung 1
Übung 2: 1. my 2. her 3. your 4. our 5. their 6. his
Übung 3: 2, 4, 6, 3, 5, 1
Übung 4: 1. f 2. e 3. a 4. b 5. d 6. c
Übung 5: 1. Who 2. Where 3. When 4. Why 5. What 6. How
Übung 6: 1. Who was that? 2. What did you do? 3. Where were they? 4. I was at the office. 5. Elvira was at home.
Übung 7: 1. six 2. eleven 3. thirty-eight 4. twenty 5. four 6. twelve 7. (one) hundred 8. fourteen 9. forty-three 10. ninety-nine 11. seventy 12. fifty-one
Übung 9: 1. It's twenty to two. 2. It's nine forty-three. 3. It's one thirty-nine. 4. It's a quarter past five. 5. It's seven fifty-five. 6. It's six thirty. 7. It's eleven o'clock. 8. It's twelve eighteen. 9. It's a quarter to eight. 10. It's a quarter past seven.
Übung 10: 1. b 2. b 3. a 4. b 5. b 6. a
Übung 11: 1. What 2. I'd like 3. with 4. Anything 5. How 6. please
Übung 12: 1. Present Continuous 2. Simple Past 3. Simple Present 4. Present Continuous 5. Present Continuous 6. Simple Past

Unit 4
4.1 Übung 1: 1. help 2. thank you 3. size 4. mother 5. sorry 6. customer
Übung 2: 1. d 2. h 3. c 4. b 5. g 6. a 7. e 8. f
Übung 3: 1. black 2. hat 3. ties 4. criminal 5. steal 6. silly

4.2 Übung 1: 1. big 2. small 3. nice 4. brown 5. old 6. perfect 7. mysterious
Übung 2: a
Übung 3: 1. coat 2. trousers 3. shirt 4. dress 5. tie 6. blouse 7. skirt

Übung 4: 1. clothes shop 2. flower shop 3. jeweller's 4. bakery 5. grocery 6. furniture shop 7. book shop

4.3 **Übung 1:** 1. shopping 2. looking 3. rings 4. answers 5. watching

Übung 2: 1. I don't say. 2. You don't reply. 3. We don't run. 4. They don't push. 5. He doesn't go. 6. She doesn't leave. 7. I don't kiss. 8. You don't speak. 9. She doesn't do. 10. We don't catch.

Übung 3: 1. He says goodbye. She says goodbye. 2. He steals my handbag. She steals my handbag. 3. He answers the phone. She answers the phone. 4. He needs a new coat. She needs a new coat.

4.4 **Übung 1:** 1. too many 2. don't know 3. can't see 4. too late 5. too tired 6. has

Übung 2: 1. fast 2. late 3. tired 4. many

Übung 3: milk, sugar, chocolate, tea, coat, coffee, flowers

Grammatik

Übung 1: 1. d 2. e 3. g 4. f 5. c 6. a 7. b

Übung 2: 1. g 2. b 3. a 4. i 5. j 6. d 7. c 8. e 9. f 10. h

Übung 3: Miss Paddington says that Inspector Hudson needs a new coat. He says that he likes his coat. Miss Paddington answers that it is old and that he has to buy a new one. He says that he doesn't like shopping. Miss Paddington replies that she knows a nice big shop. Hudson says that he doesn't like big shops. Miss Paddington says that he is impossible.

Unit 5

5.1 **Übung 1:** 1. d 2. c 3. e 4. b 5. a

Übung 2: 1. was 2. found 3. said 4. wanted 5. went 6. asked 7. smiled 8. needed 9. stayed 10. wished

Übung 3: 1. richtig 2. richtig 3. falsch 4. falsch 5. richtig 6. falsch

5.2 **Übung 1:** 1. book 2. arrive 3. How many 4. double 5. two 6. Non-smoking 7. name 8. phone number 9. See you

5.3 **Übung 1:** 1. d 2. g 3. e 4. f 5. c 6. a 7. h 8. b

Übung 2: 1. d 2. a 3. b 4. c

Übung 3: 1. I have to buy train tickets. 2. I have to book a hotel. 3. I have to organize a rental car. 4. I have to buy a guidebook. 5. I have to pack my suitcase.

Übung 4: 1. Oh no, that's too big. 2. Oh no, that's too little. 3. Oh no, it doesn't have any pictures. 4. Oh no, that's too expensive. 5. Oh yes, this is perfect! We'll take it.

5.4 **Übung 1:** Regular Verbs: wait – waited, look – looked, pay – paid, need – needed, want – wanted, say – said, ask – asked, wish – wished, print – printed
Irregular Verbs: am – was, find – found, are – were, go – went, put – put, buy – bought

Übung 2: 4, 6, 9, 3, 2, 7, 1, 5, 8

Übung 3: 1. say/says 2. go/goes 3. wait/waits 4. reply/replies 5. ask/asks 6. print/prints 7. pay/pays 8. thank/thanks

Grammatik

Übung 1: Miss Paddington and Inspector Hudson wanted to go to Edinburgh. They had to book a hotel. They had to buy train tickets. Inspector Hudson found a hotel on the Internet. He called the hotel. He went to the train station and bought the train tickets. They packed their suitcases. They bought a guidebook. They were very happy.

Übung 3: 1. have to 2. need 3. mustn't 4. has to 5. needn't 6. have to 7. needn't

Unit 6

6.1 **Übung 1:** 1. arrived, arrive 2. went, go 3. was, is 4. got, get 5. put, put 6. found, find 7. were, are 8. had, have 9. was, am

Übung 2: 1. said 2. took 3. drank 4. opened 5. started

Übung 3: 1. h 2. d 3. g 4. i 5. b 6. a 7. e 8. j 9. f 10. c

Übung 4: 1. a 2. an 3. – 4. an 5. a 6. – 7. – 8. – 9. a 10. a

6.2 Übung 1: 1. books 2. bodies 3. schools 4. leaves 5. sandwiches 6. robberies 7. policemen 8. information 9. stories 10. castles

Übung 2: 1. Are there any museums in this city? 2. Is there a sandwich in your handbag? 3. Are there any toilets in this building ? 4. Is there a castle in Edinburgh? 5. Is there an art gallery in your town?

Übung 3: 1. go to 2. see 3. find out about 4. visit 5. go to

6.3 Übung 1: 1. d 2. a 3. e 4. c 5. b

Übung 3: 1. Excuse me 2. Here 3. Go 4. left 5. end 6. right 7. on

Übung 5: 1. On 2. At 3. Past 4. Go along 5. Go straight 6. Turn

6.4 Übung 2: 1. i 2. d 3. h 4. f 5. c 6. a 7. e 8. j 9. b 10. g

Übung 3: 1. down 2. through 3. through 4. into 5. to 6. on 7. in 8. to

Übung 4: 1. on, at 2. on 3. On 4. on/at 5. in 6. at, on

Grammatik

Übung 1: The 2. – 3. a, an 4. – 5. the 6. a

Übung 2: 1. castles 2. book 3. graveyards 4. story 5. men 6. cities 7. dresses 8. mysteries

Übung 4: 1. from, to 2. next to 3. At 4. from, to 5. straight on, right, past, opposite 6. in 7. in

Wiederholung 2

Übung 1: 1. c 2. h 3. f 4. g 5. d 6. b 7. e 8. a

Übung 3: 1. big 2. handy 3. small 4. shop assistant 5. mobile phone 6. perfect 7. furniture shop 8. clothes 9. customer Lösung: inspector

Übung 4: 1. says 2. works 3. goes 4. watches 5. does 6. kisses 7. solves 8. lives 9. catches 10. drinks

Übung 5: 1. paid 2. went 3. said 4. were, had 5. stayed 6. was 7. lived

Übung 7: 5, 7, 1, 9, 2, 3, 6, 11, 10, 4, 8

Übung 8: 1. on 2. in 3. at 4. on 5. at 6. in 7. on/at 8. at 9. in

Übung 9: 1. newspapers 2. burglaries 3. thieves 4. women 5. things 6. holidays 7. galleries 8. watches 9. information 10. days

Übung 10: 1. There is 2. There are 3. There are 4. There is 5. There is 6. There is 7. There are

Übung 11: 1. into 2. next to 3. left 4. up 5. opposite 6. into 7. in

Unit 7

7.1 Übung 1: 1. head 2. ear 3. finger 4. arm 5. stomach 6. leg 7. foot 8. eye 9. nose 10. mouth 11. throat 12. heart 13. hand 14. knee 15. toe

Übung 2: 1. f 2. d 3. j 4. a 5. i 6. g 7. b 8. c 9. e 10. h

Übung 3: 1. cold 2. throat 3. running 4. cough 5. sneezing 6. headache

Übung 4: 1. Yes, he did. 2. Yes, they did. 3. Yes, he did. 4. No, she didn't. 5. No, he didn't. 6. No, they didn't.

7.2 Übung 1: 1. b 2. c 3. b 4. a

Übung 2: 1. richtig 2. richtig 3. falsch 4. richtig 5. falsch 6. richtig

Übung 3: 1. spoke to 2. lying in 3. went into 4. waited in 5. went to

7.3 Übung 1: 1. I'll 2. he'll 3. she'll 4. it'll 5. we'll 6. they'll 7. you'll

Übung 2: 1. drove 2. shook 3. went 4. switched 5. was 6. had 7. opened

Übung 3: 1. I think I'll go home. 2. I think I'll open it. 3. I think I'll have a sandwich. 4. I think I'll close the window. 5. I think I'll take a taxi.

7.4 Übung 1: 1. Twenty minutes ago. 2. For twenty minutes. 3. At 4 a.m. 4. For an hour. 5. A moment ago. 6. At 6.30 p.m.

Übung 2: 1. at 2. for 3. ago 4. for 5. for 6. At

Übung 3: 1. was standing, rang 2. were shopping, stole 3. was going, was attacked

Grammatik

Übung 1: 1. Did she meet Victor? Yes, she did. 2. Did Hudson go on holiday? Yes, he did. 3. Did I shut the window? No, I didn't. 4. Did you buy milk? Yes, you did. 5. Did he get the job? No, he didn't. 6. Did they feed the cat? No, they didn't.
Übung 2: 1. e 2. g 3. i 4. b 5. h 6. j 7. a 8. c 9. f 10. d
Übung 3: 1. The phone was ringing. 2. Elvira and Hudson were talking. 3. Miss Paddington was screaming. 4. The men were talking. 5. She was waiting at the hospital. 6. They were going to Edinburgh. 7. I was reading a thriller.
Übung 4: 1. c 2. d 3. a 4. b

Unit 8

8.1 **Übung 1:** 1. You sleep in a bed. 2. You sit in an armchair. 3. The armchair is in the living room. 4. You cook in the kitchen. 5. When I eat, I sit on a chair. 6. You brush your teeth in the bathroom.
Übung 2: 1. c 2. f 3. g 4. a 5. b 6. d 7. e
Übung 3: 1. I didn't answer the phone. 2. I think I know. 3. I need to go home. 4. Sorry, I don't remember.
Übung 4: 1. wardrobe 2. sofa 3. bed 4. chair 5. table 6. armchair

8.2 **Übung 1:** What? 2. Where? 3. Who? 4. Why? 5. Why not?
Übung 2: 1. drove 2. are talking 3. broke 4. will have 5. were sitting 6. am working 7. thought 8. was crying
Übung 3: 1. hear 2. Listen 3. listen 4. hear 5. hear 6. listen

8.3 **Übung 1:** 1. the moment after 2. at the moment 3. at the last moment 4. a moment later 5. a moment
Übung 2: 6 x had to
Übung 3: 1. bedroom 2. spare bedroom 3. living room 4. corridor 5. kitchen 6. bathroom
Übung 4: 1. On Saturday she has to go shopping. 2. Tonight he has to study English. 3. You have to listen to your mailbox. 4. She has to go to the toilet. 5. They have to call Elvira at 8 p.m.

8.4 **Übung 1:** 1. f 2. c 3. a 4. d 5. b 6. e
Übung 2: 1. living room 2. holiday 3. but 4. careful 5. hurt 6. later 7. office 8. reports 9. because 10. shop 11. maybe 12. remember
Übung 3: 1. the investigation 2. to talk 3. her mobile 4. not available 5. a police car 6. Ann's flat 7. the living room

Grammatik

Übung 1: 1. I didn't find Ann Watson. 2. They didn't look for hairs. 3. The police were not trying to find the shop. 4. Inspector Hudson didn't hear Victor's voice. 5. He saw me. 6. They were listening to the radio. 7. You're a good inspector. 8. We weren't frightened. 9. She's a housekeeper. 10. Elvira liked tea.
Übung 2: 1. l 2. i 3. h 4. p 5. b 6. c 7. m 8. d 9. a 10. f 11. e 12. n 13. k 14. j 15. g 16. o

Unit 9

9.1 **Übung 1:** 1. was waiting 2. has murdered 3. said 4. has attacked 5. has set 6. has kidnapped 7. is
Übung 2: 1. write, wrote, written 2. find, found, found 3. call, called, called 4. go, went, gone 5. say, said, said 6. come, came, come 7. see, saw, seen 8. eat, ate, eaten 9. be, was, been 10. do, did, done
Übung 3: 1. has written 2. has gone 3. have found 4. has been 5. have seen 6. have had

9.2 **Übung 1:** 1. any 2. any 3. some, any 4. some, some 5. any(thing) 6. Some
Übung 2: 1. Has the Inspector gone to Brighton? – Yes, he went there yesterday. 2. Have you found any witnesses yet? – Yes, we have found some people who saw the car. 3. Have you seen Elvira? – Yes, I saw her three days ago.

Übung 3: 1. h 2. i 3. b 4. e 5. f 6. a 7. c 8. d 9. j 10. g

9.3 Übung 1: 1. haven't you? 2. hasn't she? 3. did they? 4. didn't they? 5. can he? 6. has it?

Übung 2: 1. which 2. who 3. who 4. which 5. who 6. which

9.4 Übung 1: 1. Past Continuous 2. Simple Past 3. Present Perfect 4. Present Simple 5. Future 6. Present Continuous

Übung 2: 1. c 2. d 3. e 4. b 5. a

Übung 3: 1. short, grey, watching, Miss Paddington 2. wears, coat, Scotland Yard, solves, Inspector James Hudson 3. grey, moustache, big, Sir Reginald 4. red, tall, insurance, crime, Elvira Elliot 5. thin, black, hat, commits

Grammatik

Übung 1: 1. d 2. c 3. b 4. a

Übung 2: 1. up 2. off 3. on

Unit 10

10.1 Übung 1: 1. c 2. e 3. b 4. f 5. a 6. d

Übung 2: 1. slowly 2. loudly 3. quietly 4. carefully 5. badly 6. suddenly

Übung 3: 1. loudly 2. slowly 3. badly 4. Suddenly 5. quietly 6. carefully

10.2 Übung 1: 1. big, bigger, biggest 2. bad, worse, worst 3. intelligent, more intelligent, most intelligent 4. good, better, best 5. old, older, oldest 6. nice, nicer, nicest 7. young, younger, youngest 8. beautiful, more beautiful, most beautiful 9. early, earlier, earliest

Übung 2: 1. have to 2. too tired 3. too fast 4. too many 5. at home

10.3 Übung 1: 1. threw, broke 2. through 3. turned 4. left 5. some 6. any

Übung 2: "You had murdered Constable Watson because she had been helping the investigation. Then you had brought Elvira to Brighton. Elvira had left the flat to buy bread. You had left the flat a moment later. You had run to the rented Mercedes. You had driven to the bakery, then you had told Elvira to get into the car. Later you had given her drugs and had brought her back to the flat."

Übung 3: 1. d 2. f 3. g 4. a 5. h 6. b 7. c 8. e

10.4 Übung 1: 1. a) going to do b) going to go 2. a) going to do b) going to have 3. a) going to do b) going to leave 4. a) going to do b) going to relax

Grammatik

Übung 1: 1. as slow as 2. as good as 3. as big as 4. as interesting as 5. as long as

Übung 2: 1. fitter 2. lazier 3. older 4. worse 5. more intelligent

Übung 3: 1. smartest 2. prettiest 3. most expensive 4. most delicious 5. worst

Übung 4: 1. falsch 2. richtig 3. richtig 4. falsch 5. richtig 6. richtig 7. falsch 8. richtig

Wiederholung 3

Übung 1: 1. Did Hudson stay in Edinburgh? 2. Did they find any clue? 3. Did you go to the doctor's?

Übung 2: 1. ago 2. At 3. For 4. For 5. ago

Übung 3: 1. The glass was breaking. 2. I was reading a crime story. 3. They were going on holiday. 4. Hudson was waiting downstairs.

Übung 4: 1. hear 2. Listen 3. Listen 4. hear

Übung 5: 1. Tomorrow I have to read this crime story. 2. Tonight you have to have a shower. 3. Next week we have to buy new clothes. 4. Tomorrow morning he has to go to work. 5. At 3.30 they have to catch the train. 6. Later she has to feed the dog.

Übung 6: 1. The inspector didn't buy a new coat. 2. We didn't find a clue. 3. I wasn't drinking coffee. 4. They didn't go to Brighton. 5. She didn't come to the party. 6. Sir Reginald didn't get hurt.

Übung 7: 1. b 2. a 3. b 4. b

Übung 8: 1. some 2. some, some 3. any… 4. any, some 5. any

Übung 9: 1. Inspector Hudson is a policeman. He works at Scotland Yard. He solves crime. He's got dark hair and wears a brown coat and hat. He likes Elvira Elliot.
2. Elvira Elliot is an insurance investigator. She works at an insurance company. She's got long red hair. She's thin and tall. She likes to solve crime, too.
3. Miss Paddington is Inspector Hudson's housekeeper. She is short and fat. She's got grey hair. She likes watching crime movies.
Übung 10: 1. loudly 2. careful 3. polite 4. well 5. fast
Übung 11: 1. bigger 2. reddest 3. most delicious 4. worse 5. more expensive
Übung 12: 1. (I)'m going to go/will go 2. going to meet 3. (I)'ll have 4. going to do

Abschlusstest
Übung 1: Monday, Tuesday, Wednesday, Thursday, Friday, Saturday, Sunday
Übung 2: 1. his 2. my 3. her 4. our 5. their 6. his
Übung 3: 1. Who 2. Where 3. When 4. What 5. Why
Übung 4: 1. a quarter to one 2. eleven o'clock 3. five minutes to seven 4. half past one 5. a quarter past three 6. ten minutes past eight 7. twenty minutes to four 8. ten minutes to nine 9. twenty minutes past ten 10. half past eleven
Übung 5: 1. I am working. 2. We are talking. 3. He is eating and drinking. 5. She is sitting in a café. 6. They are going on holiday.
Übung 6: 1. d 2. e 3. f 4. c 5. b 6. a
Übung 7: 1. does 2. goes 3. sees 4. kisses 5. leaves 6. plays 7. hears 8. pushes 9. says 10. watches
Übung 8: never, seldom, sometimes, often, always
Übung 9: 1. was 2. said 3. wanted 4. did 5. went 6. paid 7. were 8. saw 9. came
Übung 10: 1. stories 2. sandwiches 3. policemen 4. burglaries 5. information 6. messages 7. women 8. thieves 9. galleries 10. taxis
Übung 11: 1. wund 2. Magen 3. Husten 4. Rachen 5. Kopfschmerzen 6. Knie
Übung 12: 1. We were talking. 2. I was waiting. 3. Elvira was meeting me. 4. They were going on holiday. 5. He was reading a book.
Übung 13: 1. works 2. broke 3. I'm going to have 4. I'll have 5. are learning
Übung 14: 1. Biegen Sie nach rechts ab. 2. An der Ampel 3. Gehen Sie die Queen Street entlang. 4. Links 5. Am Ende der Straße 6. Nach dem Scott Monument 7. Biegen Sie nach rechts ab. 8. Biegen Sie bei der zweiten (Straße) links ab.
Übung 15: 1. write, wrote, written 2. find, found, found 3. go, went, gone 4. eat, ate, eaten 5. see, saw, seen 6. be, was, been 7. talk, talked, talked
Übung 16: 1. older 2. best 3. oldest 4. more beautiful 5. best 6. most beautiful 7. worst 8. better
Übung 17: 1. f 2. e 3. g 4. a 5. d 6. b 7. c

GRAMMATIK

DER ARTIKEL

Ob der unbestimmte Artikel **a** oder **an** benutzt wird, hängt vom ersten Laut des folgenden Wortes ab: **a** vor Konsonanten, **an** vor einem Vokal.

***a s**inger* *an **o**pera singer*

Der bestimmte Artikel ist immer **the**. Allerdings wird er vor einem Wort, das mit einem Vokal beginnt, mit langem ***i*** [ðiː] ausgesprochen. Vor Berufsbezeichnungen wird im Englischen immer der unbestimmte Artikel verwendet: *Inspector Hudson is **a** policeman.*

DAS SUBSTANTIV

Im Englischen werden Substantive in der Regel klein geschrieben. Ausnahmen, die immer groß geschrieben werden, sind Eigennamen und Titel (z. B. *Inspector Hudson*), Wochentage (z. B. *Monday*) und Monate (z. B. *July*), Länder (z. B. *Germany*) und Institutionen (z. B. *Scotland Yard*).

Pluralbildung

Im Normalfall wird die Pluralform durch Anhängen der Endung **-s** gebildet (z. B. *door – door**s***).
Ausnahmen:
Nach **-s**, **-ss**, **-sh**, **-ch** oder **-x** am Wortende wird **-es** angehängt (z. B. *watch – wat**ches**; bus – bu**ses**; tax – ta**xes***).
-y nach einem Konsonanten am Wortende wird zu **-ies** (z. B. *hobby – hobb**ies***).
-f am Wortende wird zu **-ves** (z. B. *thief – thie**ves***).

! Einige englische Substantive besitzen keine Pluralform, z. B. *information, news* oder *knowledge*.

Unregelmäßige Pluralformen

!

man (Mann)	*men*	*tooth* (Zahn)	*teeth*
woman (Frau)	*women*	*sheep* (Schaf)	*sheep*
child (Kind)	*children*	*fish* (Fisch)	*fish*
foot (Fuß)	*feet*	*tomato* (Tomate)	*tomatoes*

DIE PRONOMEN

DAS PERSONALPRONOMEN

Subjekt	Objekt	Subjekt	Objekt
I	*me*	*we*	*us*
you	*you*	*you*	*you*
he	*him*	*they*	*them*
she	*her*		
it	*it*		

Die Objektform kann sowohl dem deutschen Dativ als auch dem Akkusativ entsprechen:

*I give the book **to him**.*	*I give **him** the book.*	Ich gebe **ihm** das Buch. (Dativ)
*He calls **her**.*		Er ruft **sie**. (Akkusativ)

DAS POSSESSIVPRONOMEN

Possessivpronomen drücken den Besitz oder die Zugehörigkeit aus (z. B. ***his** house*). Die substantivischen Possessivpronomen werden verwendet, um eine Wiederholung des Substantivs zu vermeiden:

*Is this **your handbag**?* *Yes, this is **mine**. (= **my handbag**)*

adjektivisch	substantivisch	adjektivisch	substantivisch
I	*my*	*we*	*our*
you	*your*	*you*	*your*
he	*his*	*they*	*theirs*
she	*her*		
it	*its*		

DAS DEMONSTRATIVPRONOMEN

Singular	Plural	
this	***these***	weisen auf räumlich/zeitlich nahe Objekte hin
that	***those***	verweisen auf räumlich/zeitlich entferntere Objekte

***This** book is more interesting than **that** book.* — **Dieses** Buch ist interessanter als **jenes** Buch (**dort**).

DAS ADJEKTIV

Adjektive vermitteln Informationen über Menschen oder Dinge. Sie sind also beschreibende Wörter. Im Englischen sind die Adjektive unveränderlich.

*She's an **intelligent** woman. It's a **nice** day. Those flowers are **lovely**.*
*The party is **wonderful**.*

Steigerung

Ein- und zweisilbige Adjektive; Adjektive mit mehr als zwei Silben werden mit ***more/most*** gesteigert, Endkonsonanten werden verdoppelt.

	Komparativ	Superlativ
long	*longer*	*longest*
beautiful	***more** beautiful*	***most** beautiful*

Unregelmäßige Adjektive

!	Komparativ	Superlativ
good (gut)	*better*	*best*
bad (schlecht)	*worse*	*worst*
much (viel)	*more*	*most*

many (viele)	*more*	*most*
little (wenig)	*less*	*least*
little (klein)	*smaller*	*smallest*
far (weit)	*further*	*furthest*

DAS ADVERB

Adverbien bestimmen ein Verb genauer. Im Englischen werden die Adverbien gebildet, indem ***-ly*** an das Adjektiv angehängt wird (z. B. *slow* – *slow**ly***). Besonderheiten:
Endet das Adjektiv auf ***-e***, entfällt dieses ***-e*** und das ***-ly*** wird an den Wortstamm gehängt, z. B. *terrib**le*** – *terrib**ly***.
Bei Adjektiven, die auf ***-y*** enden, wird ***-ily*** angehängt, z. B. *eas**y*** – *eas**ily***.
Endet das Adjektiv auf ***-ic*** wird ***-ally*** angehängt, z. B. *basic* – *basic**ally***

Manchmal haben Adjektiv und Adverb dieselbe Form. Die wichtigsten Beispiele sind:

Adjektiv	Adverb	
fast	*fast*	(schnell)
hard	*hard*	(hart, schwer)
long	*long*	(lange)
early	*early*	(früh)
late	*late*	(spät)
daily	*daily*	(täglich)

DAS VERB

Die Verben *to be*, *to have* und *to do*

Die Verben ***do***, ***be*** und ***have*** können sowohl Vollverben (Verben, die alleine das Prädikat einen Satzes bilden können: Ich **esse** eine Banane.) als auch Hilfsverben sein. Als Hilfsverben werden mit Ihnen die Fragen, die Verneinung und alle zusammengesetzten Zeiten gebildet.

to be

Infinitiv	Simple Past	Past Participle
to be	*was/were*	*been*
sein	war/waren	gewesen

Simple Present		Kurzform	Verneinung	Kurzform
I am	ich bin	*I'm*	*I am not*	*I'm not*
you are	du bist	*you're*	*you are not*	*you aren't*
he is	er ist	*he's*	*he is not*	*he isn't*
she is	sie ist	*she's*	*she is not*	*she isn't*
it is	es ist	*it's*	*it is not*	*it isn't*
we are	wir sind	*we're*	*we are not*	*we aren't*
you are	ihr seid	*you're*	*you are not*	*you aren't*
they are	sie sind	*they're*	*they are not*	*they aren't*

Simple Past			Verneinung	Kurzform
I was	ich war		*I was not*	*I wasn't*
you were	du warst		*you were not*	*you weren't*
he was	er war		*he was not*	*he wasn't*
she was	sie war		*she was not*	*she wasn't*
it was	es war		*it was not*	*it wasn't*
we were	wir waren		*we were not*	*we weren't*
you were	ihr wart		*you were not*	*you weren't*
they were	sie waren		*they were not*	*they weren't*

to have

Infinitiv		Simple Past	Past Participle	
have	haben	*had* hatte	*had* gehabt	
Simple Present		Kurzform	Verneinung	Kurzform
I have	ich habe	*I've*	*I have not*	*I haven't*
you have	du hast	*you've*	*you have not*	*you haven't*
he has	er hat	*he's*	*he has not*	*he hasn't*
she has	sie hat	*she's*	*she has not*	*she hasn't*
it has	es hat	*it's*	*it has not*	*it hasn`t*
we have	wir haben	*we've*	*we have not*	*we haven't*
you have	ihr habt	*you've*	*you have not*	*you haven't*
they have	sie haben	*they've*	*they have not*	*they haven't*
Imperfekt		Kurzform	Verneinung	Kurzform
I had	ich hatte	*I'd*	*I had not*	*I hadn't*
you had	du hattest	*you'd*	*you had not*	*you hadn't*
he had	er hatte	*he'd*	*he had not*	*he hadn't*
she had	sie hatte	*she'd*	*she had not*	*she hadn't*
it had	es hatte	–	*it had not*	*it hadn't*
we had	wir hatten	*we'd*	*we had not*	*we hadn't*
you had	ihr hattet	*you'd*	*you had not*	*you hadn't*
they had	sie hatten	*they'd*	*they had not*	*they hadn't*

to do

Infinitiv		Simple Past	Past Participle	
do	tun	*did* tat	*done* getan	
Simple Past		Kurzform	Verneinung	Kurzform
I did	ich tat	–	*I did not*	*I didn't*
you did	du tatst	–	etc.	etc.

VOLLVERBEN

Bei regelmäßigen Vollverben wird in der 3. Person Singular (*he/she/it*) der Gegenwart ein ***-s*** an das Verb anhängen (z. B. *he/she/it works*). Endet das Verb auf ***-o*** (*to go, to do*) wird ein ***-es*** angehängt.
Die beiden Vergangenheitsformen **Simple Past** und **Past Participle** werden durch Anhängen der Endung ***-ed*** an den Infinitiv gebildet (z. B. *work – work**ed** – work**ed***). Das Present Perfect wird gebildet mit ***have/has*** + **Past Participle**.
Die sogenannten Verlaufsformen **Present Continuous** und **Past Continuous** werden mit einer Form von ***to be*** + ***-ing***-Form des Verbes gebildet (z. B. *is/are working; was/were working*).

Das Verb *to work* (arbeiten)

Infinitiv	Simple Past	Past Participle
work	*worked*	*worked*
Simple Present		Verneinung
I work	ich arbeite	*I don't work*
you work	du arbeitest	*you don't work*
he/she/it works	er/sie/es arbeitet	*he/she/it* ***doesn't*** *work*
we work	wir arbeiten	*we don't work*
you work	ihr arbeitet	*you don't work*
they work	sie arbeiten	*they don't work*
Present Continuous		Verneinung
I am working	ich arbeite (gerade)	*I'm not working*
you are working	du arbeitest (gerade)	*you aren't working*
he/she/it is working	er/sie/es arbeitet (gerade)	*he/she/it* ***isn't*** *working*
we are working	wir arbeiten (gerade)	*we aren't working*
you are working	ihr arbeitet (gerade)	*you aren't working*
they are working	sie arbeiten (gerade)	*they aren't working*
Simple Past		Verneinung
I worked	ich arbeitete	*I didn't work*
you worked	du arbeitetest	*you didn't work*
he/she/it worked	er/sie/es arbeitete	*he/she/it didn't work*
we worked	wir arbeiteten	*we didn't work*
you worked	ihr arbeitetet	*you didn't work*
they worked	sie arbeiteten	*they didn't work*
Past Continuous		Verneinung
I was working	ich arbeitete (gerade)	*I'm wasn't working*
you were working	du arbeitetest (gerade)	*you weren't working*

he/she/it was working	er/sie/es arbeitete (gerade)	*he/she/it* ***wasn't*** *working*
we were working	wir arbeiteten (gerade)	*we weren't working*
you were working	ihr arbeitetet (gerade)	*you weren't working*
they were working	sie arbeiteten (gerade)	*they weren't working*
Present Perfect		Verneinung
I have worked	ich habe gearbeitet	*I haven't worked*
you have worked	du hast gearbeitet	*you haven't worked*
he/she/it has worked	er/sie/es hat gearbeitet	*he/she/it* ***hasn't*** *worked*
we have worked	wir haben gearbeitet	*we haven't worked*
you have worked	ihr habt gearbeitet	*you haven't worked*
they have worked	sie haben gearbeitet	*they haven't worked*
will-Future		Verneinung
I will work	ich werde arbeiten	*I won't work*
you will work	du wirst arbeiten	*you won't work*
he/she/it will work	er/sie/es wird arbeiten	*he/she/it won't work*
we will work	wir werden arbeiten	*we won't work*
you will work	ihr werdet arbeiten	*you won't work*
they will work	sie werden arbeiten	*they won't work*

Der Imperativ

Man benutzt den Imperativ für Befehle und Aufforderungen. Er wird mit dem Infinitiv (der Grundform) des Verbs gebildet und mit ***don't*** verneint:

Come *home!* — Komm/kommt/kommen Sie nach Hause!
Don't come *home!* — Komm/kommt/kommen Sie nicht nach Hause!

DIE UHRZEIT

Im Englischen geht man nicht nach der 24-Stunden-Uhr, sondern verwendet die Zahlen von eins bis zwölf zusammen mit ***a.m.*** (vor zwölf Uhr mittags) und ***p.m.*** (nach zwölf Uhr mittags):

8:00 Uhr — *8.00* ***a.m.*** — 20:00 Uhr — *8.00* ***p.m.***

Wenn ohnehin klar ist, um welche Tageszeit es sich handelt, kann man die Angabe ***a.m./p.m.*** weglassen.

Die 30 Minuten **nach** der vollen Stunde sind ***past***, die 29 Minuten **vor** der vollen Stunde ***to***.

! Auch **halb** ist **nach**! **Halb vier** heißt also ***half past three***.

Der Zusatz ***o'clock*** wird nur bei vollen Stunden verwendet, also z.B. bei *8.00 = eight o'clock*. Man kann die Uhrzeit auch „digital" ausdrücken.

a quarter to two = one forty-five
a quarter past seven = seven fifteen
half past four = four thirty

DIE UNREGELMÄSSIGEN VERBEN

Infinitive	Simple Past	Past Participle	Übersetzung
arise	arose	arisen	aufkommen
awake	awoke	awoken	aufwachen
be	was/were	been	sein
bear	bore	borne/born	tragen
beat	beat	beaten	schlagen
become	became	become	werden
begin	began	begun	anfangen
bend	bent	bent	biegen
bet	bet/betted	bet/betted	wetten
bid	bid	bid	bieten
bind	bound	bound	binden
bite	bit	bitten	beißen
bleed	bled	bled	bluten
blow	blew	blown	blasen
break	broke	broken	brechen
breed	bred	bred	züchten
bring	brought	brought	bringen
build	built	built	bauen
burn	burnt/burned	burnt/burned	brennen
burst	burst	burst	bersten
buy	bought	bought	kaufen
can	could	-	können
cast	cast	cast	werfen
catch	caught	caught	fangen
choose	chose	chosen	auswählen
cleave	clove/cleft	cloven/cleft	spalten
cling	clung	clung	haften
come	came	come	kommen
cost	cost	cost	kosten
creep	crept	crept	kriechen
cut	cut	cut	schneiden
deal	dealt	dealt	handeln/geben
dig	dug	dug	graben
do	did	done	tun
draw	drew	drawn	ziehen/zeichnen
dream	dreamt/dreamed	dreamt/dreamed	träumen
drink	drank	drunk	trinken
drive	drove	driven	fahren
eat	ate	eaten	essen
fall	fell	fallen	fallen
feed	fed	fed	füttern
feel	felt	felt	fühlen
fight	fought	fought	kämpfen
find	found	found	finden
flee	fled	fled	flüchten

fly	flew	flown	fliegen
forbid	forbade	forbidden	verbieten
forget	forgot	forgotten	vergessen
freeze	froze	frozen	(ge)frieren
get	got	got (US gotten)	bekommen
give	gave	given	geben
go	went	gone	gehen
grow	grew	grown	wachsen
hang	hung	hung	hängen
have	had	had	haben
hear	heard	heard	hören
hide	hid	hid	(sich) verstecken
hit	hit	hit	schlagen
hold	held	held	halten
hurt	hurt	hurt	verletzen
keep	kept	kept	behalten
know	knew	known	wissen/kennen
lay	laid	laid	legen
lead	led	led	führen
lean	leant/leaned	leant/leaned	lehnen
learn	learnt/learned	learnt/learned	lernen
leave	left	left	(ver)lassen
lend	lent	lent	(aus)leihen
let	let	let	lassen
lie	lay	lain	liegen
light	lit	lit	anzünden
lose	lost	lost	verlieren
make	made	made	machen
may	might	-	dürfen
mean	meant	meant	bedeuten
meet	met	met	treffen/ begegnen
pay	paid	paid	bezahlen
put	put	put	setzen/stellen/ legen
quit	quit	quit	verlassen
read	read	read	lesen
ride	rode	ridden	reiten
ring	rang	rung	läuten/klingeln
rise	rose	risen	sich erheben
run	ran	run	laufen/rennen
say	said	said	sagen
see	saw	seen	sehen
sell	sold	sold	verkaufen
send	sent	sent	senden
set	set	set	setzen/stellen
sew	sewed	sewn	nähen
shake	shook	shaken	schütteln/wackeln
shave	shaved	shaved/shaven	rasieren
shed	shed	shed	vergießen
shine	shone	shone	scheinen
shoot	shot	shot	(er)schießen

show	showed	shown	zeigen
shrink	shrank	shrunk	schrumpfen
shut	shut	shut	schließen
sing	sang	sung	singen
sink	sank	sunk	sinken
sit	sat	sat	sitzen
slay	slayed	slain	erschlagen
sleep	slept	slept	schlagen
slide	slid	slid	rutschen
sling	slung	slung	schlingen
slit	slit	slit	schlitzen
smell	smelt/smelled	smelt/smelled	riechen
speak	spoke	spoken	sprechen
speed	sped	sped	eilen
spell	spelt/spelled	spelt/spelled	buchstabieren
spend	spent	spent	ausgeben/ verbringen (Zeit)
spin	span	spun	drehen
spit	spat	spat	spucken
split	split	split	spalten
spoil	spoilt/spoiled	spoilt/spoiled	verderben
spread	spread	spread	(sich) ausbreiten
spring	sprang	sprung	springen
stand	stood	stood	stehen
steal	stole	stolen	stehlen
stick	stuck	stuck	kleben/stecken
sting	stang	stung	stechen
stink	stank	stunk	stinken
strike	struck	struck	schlagen
strive	strove	striven	anstreben
swear	swore	sworn	schwören
sweep	swept	swept	fegen
swell	swelled	swollen/swelled	schwellen
swim	swam	swum	schwimmen
swing	swang	swung	schwingen
take	took	taken	nehmen
teach	taught	taught	lehren/unterrichten
tell	told	told	sagen/erzählen
think	thought	thought	denken
throw	threw	thrown	werfen
understand	understood	understood	verstehen
wake	woke	woken	wecken/aufwachen
wear	wore	worn	tragen
weep	wept	wept	weinen
win	won	won	gewinnen
wind	wound	wound	(sich) winden/ kurbeln
write	wrote	written	schreiben

Abkürzungen

Pl.	Plural
Sg.	Singular

Im Glossar wurden alle Wörter, angeordnet nach Lektionen, in alphabetischer Reihenfolge aufgeführt. Alle Verben sind mit „to" gekennzeichnet. Einzelne unregelmäßige Verbformen wurden in das Glossar aufgenommen. Dahinter in Klammern finden Sie die Grundform des jeweiligen Verbs. Auch bei den Kurzformen wird auf die entsprechende ausführliche Form hingewiesen. Unregelmäßig gebildete Pluralformen stehen bei den Singularformen der Substantive.
Sie können diese Liste auf vielfache Art und Weise verwenden: zum Nachschlagen während des Lesens der Kapitel, beim Bearbeiten der Übungen oder zum systematischen Auswendiglernen der Vokabeln. Auf CD 2 (ab Track 29) können Sie die Aussprache der Wörter anhören und trainieren. Und Sie können mit Hilfe der CD lektionsweise die gelernten Vokabeln überprüfen.

Unit 1 (CD 2-29)

a	ein/eine
about	über
address	Adresse
alphabet	Alphabet
am (→ to be)	(ich) bin
an	ein/eine (vor Vokalen)
and	und
to answer	antworten
are (→ to be)	(wir/ihr/sie) sind
to ask	fragen
at	auf, an, um, (bei Anschrift:) in
back	zurück
to be	sein
big	groß
bill	Rechnung
black	schwarz
to boil	kochen
boiled	gekocht, (Ei:) hartgekocht
boss	Chef(in)
breakfast	Frühstück
to bring	(mit)bringen
burglar	Einbrecher(in)
burglary	Einbruch
to burgle	einbrechen
business card	Visitenkarte
butter	Butter
can	können
cannot	nicht können
can't (→ cannot)	nicht können
card	(Visiten-)Karte
caviar	Kaviar
champagne	Champagner
clever	clever, schlau

to come	kommen
to come in	hereinkommen
crime	Verbrechen
criminal	Verbrecher(in)
criminology	Kriminologie
day	Tag
delicious	schmackhaft, lecker
dining room	Esszimmer
to do	machen, tun
door	Tür
dress	Kleid
to drink	trinken
to eat	essen
egg	Ei
electricity	Strom
every	jede/r/s
everybody	jede/r
famous	berühmt
fine	gut
for	für
Friday	Freitag
friend	Freund(in)
from	von
to get	holen, bekommen
to get out	aussteigen
to give	geben
glass, glasses (*Pl.*)	Glas
to go	gehen
good	gut, lecker
green	grün
hair	Haar(e)
hand	Hand
happy	glücklich
has (→ to have)	(er/sie/es) hat
to have	haben
he	er
to hear	hören
hello	hallo
to help	helfen
her	ihr, sie
here	hier
here's (→ here is)	hier ist, das ist
he's (→ he is)	er ist
him	ihn, ihm
his	sein
house	Haus
housekeeper	Haushälter(in)
how	wie
How are you?	Wie geht es Ihnen/dir/euch?
I	ich
I'm (→ I am)	ich bin
in	in
inspector	Inspektor
insurance	Versicherung
insurance investigator	Versicherungs-agent(in)
intelligent	intelligent
interesting	interessant
into	hinein, in
to investigate	ermitteln
investigation	Ermittlung
investigator	Ermittler(in)
invitation	Einladung
is (→ to be)	(er/sie/es) ist
it	es
it's (→ it is)	es ist
jewellery	Schmuck
jewellery shop	Juweliergeschäft
kitchen	Küche
to know	kennen

last	letzte/r/s
to laugh	lachen
letter	Brief
to like	mögen
like	wie (bei Vergleichen)
to live	leben, wohnen
living room	Wohnzimmer
long	lang/e/s
to look	(an)sehen, (an)schauen
to look like	aussehen wie
lovely	hübsch, freundlich
mail	Post
man, men (*Pl.*)	Mann
many	viel/e/s
maybe	vielleicht
me	mir, mich
to meet	treffen
Miss	Fräulein
Monday	Montag
more	mehr
morning	Morgen
most	meist/e/n
music	Musik
my	mein/e
name	Name
newspaper	Zeitung
next to	neben
nice	schön
of	von
office	Büro, Kanzlei
often	oft, häufig
oh	oh (Ausruf)
OK	okay
on	auf, in, (bei Datum:) am
one	ein/e/s
to open	öffnen
opera	Oper
opera singer	Opernsänger(in)
our	unser
out	raus
party, parties (*Pl.*)	Party, Feier, Fest
people (*nur Pl.*)	Leute
person	Person
phone	Telefon
piano	Klavier
to play	spielen
p.m.	nachmittags; nach 12 Uhr mittags
police	Polizei
policeman	Polizist
professor	Professor(in)
to read	lesen
really	wirklich
red	rot
to report	berichten (von)
room	Zimmer
Saturday	Samstag
to say	sagen
Scotland Yard	Londoner Polizeibehörde
to see	sehen
to shake	schütteln
to shake hands	sich die Hand geben
she	sie
she's (→ she is)	sie ist
shop	Laden
singer	Sänger(in)

small talk	Geplauder, Small Talk
to smile	lächeln
Simple Present	Gegenwart (Grammatik)
sir	Herr, Sir
so	so, sehr
to solve	lösen, aufklären
solved	gelöst, aufgeklärt
sometimes	manchmal
to stand	stehen
to stop	aufhören, anhalten
street	Straße
to study	studieren, lernen; untersuchen
Sunday	Sonntag
to take	nehmen
to talk	sprechen, reden, sich unterhalten
taxi	Taxi
tea	(Schwarz-)Tee
team	Team, Gruppe
thanks	danke
that	jene/r/s; der, die, das
that's (→ that is)	das ist
the	der, die, das
their	ihr
them	sie
there	dort, da
The Times	The Times (engl. Tageszeitung)
they	sie (*Pl.*)
they're (→ they are)	sie sind
to think	denken, glauben
this	diese/s/r, dies
Thursday	Donnerstag
time	Zeit
to	zu, nach; (bei Brief:) an, für
toast	Toast
together	zusammen
tonight	heute Abend
too	auch
Tuesday	Dienstag
two	zwei
university	Universität
very	sehr
to wave	winken
we	wir
to wear	tragen (Kleidung)
Wednesday	Mittwoch
we're (→ we are)	wir sind
what	was
when	wenn, wann
with	mit
wonderful	wunderbar, herrlich
work	Arbeit
to work	arbeiten
you	du, ihr, Sie
your	dein/e/s, euer/eure/s, Ihr/e/s
you're (→ you are)	du bist

Unit 2 2-30

about	über, um
afternoon	Nachmittag
again	wieder, noch einmal
a.m.	vormittags, vor 12 Uhr mittags

to answer	antworten, abheben (Telefonhörer)
around	um, herum
at home	zu Hause, daheim
book	Buch
both	beide
but	aber, jedoch
bye	(auf) Wiedersehen
café	Café
call	Anruf
to call	rufen, anrufen
caller	Anrufer(in)
careful	vorsichtig
cinema	Kino
coat	Mantel
coffee	Kaffee
constable	Wachtmeister(in), Polizeibeamter, -beamtin
criminal	Kriminelle(r)
danger	Gefahr
dangerous	gefährlich
deep	tief
did (→ to do)	tat, hat getan, machte, hat gemacht
does (→ to do)	tun, machen
do not	nicht tun
don't (→ do not)	nicht tun
eight	acht
eighteen	achtzehn
eleven	elf
empty	leer
fifteen	fünfzehn
to find	finden
five	fünf
four	vier
fourteen	vierzehn
frightened	verängstigt
frightening	beängstigend
goodbye	auf Wiedersehen
great	großartig
to hang	hängen
to hang up	auflegen (Telefonhörer)
to have to + Infinitiv	müssen
hi	hallo
home	Heim, Zuhause
to install	installieren, einrichten
joke	Witz
knock	Klopfen
to know	wissen
late	spät (dran), verspätet
later	später
murder	Mord
to murder	ermorden, umbringen
murderer	Mörder(in)
next	nächste/r/s
nine	neun
nineteen	neunzehn
no	nein; nicht; kein
not	nicht
notebook	Notizbuch
now	jetzt, gleich, sofort
o'clock	Uhr (bei Zeitangabe von vollen Stunden)
of course	natürlich, selbstverständlich, sicher

or	oder
phone call	Anruf
phone tap	Telefonwanze
please	bitte
problem	Problem
to put on	anziehen
quiet	ruhig, still
reply	Antwort, Erwiderung
to reply	antworten, entgegnen
to ring	klingeln, läuten
safe	Safe, Tresor
safe	sicher
seven	sieben
seventeen	siebzehn
shall	sollen, werden
shocked	erschrocken
silence	Stille
Simple Past	Vergangenheit (Grammatik)
to sit	sitzen
six	sechs
sixteen	sechzehn
somebody	jemand
something	etwas
to speak	sprechen, reden
speaking	am Sprechen, (Telefon:) am Apparat
to start	beginnen, anfangen, starten
strange	seltsam
suddenly	plötzlich
telephone	Telefon
to tell	erzählen
ten	zehn
that	dass
these	diese (hier)
thirteen	dreizehn
those	jene (dort)
three	drei
time	Uhr(zeit)
twelve	zwölf
twenty	zwanzig
voice	Stimme
to want	möchten, wollen
was (→ to be)	war, ist gewesen
were (→ to be)	waren, sind gewesen
where	wo
which	welche/r/s
who	wer
why	warum
will	werden
window	Fenster
woman, women (*Pl.*)	Frau
to worry	sich Sorgen machen
to write	schreiben

Unit 3 2-31

all	alles, alle, ganze/r/s, ganz
all the time	die ganze Zeit, immer
another	noch eine(r), ein(e) andere(r)
anything	(irgend) etwas, jedes, alles

to arrive	ankommen
bad	schlecht
bag	(Hand-)Tasche
beer	Bier
blueberry	Blaubeere
cake	Kuchen
car	Auto
chocolate	Schokolade
concert	Konzert
crime story	Krimi
cup	Tasse
to drive	fahren, lenken (Auto)
to drive off	wegfahren
eighty	achtzig
else	sonst, außerdem
enemy	Feind(in)
English	Englisch
everyone	jede/r
to feel	fühlen
fifty	fünfzig
for	hier: nach
forty	vierzig
full	voll
to get	bringen, holen, bekommen
to go shopping	einkaufen, bummeln gehen
half	halb
help	Hilfe
I'd (→ I would)	ich würde
is gone (→ to go)	hier: ist weg, ist verschwunden
just	nur, einfach
to leave	verlassen
milk	Milch
minute	Minute
moment	Moment
money	Geld
muffin	Muffin
museum	Museum
to need	müssen; benötigen, brauchen
ninety	neunzig
nobody can	niemand darf
of	von
one hundred	einhundert
open	offen, geöffnet
past	nach (bei Uhrzeit)
to phone	anrufen
piece	Stück
pound	Pfund (Währung)
Present Continuous	Verlaufsform der Gegenwart (Grammatik)
quarter	Viertel
seventy	siebzig
shopping	Einkauf(en)
to shout	rufen
to sit down	hinsetzen
sixty	sechzig
sorry	Entschuldigung
to stand up	aufstehen
to steal	stehlen
stolen	gestohlen
sugar	(Würfel-)Zucker
theft	Diebstahl
thief, thieves (*Pl.*)	Dieb(in)
thirty	dreißig
to	vor (bei Uhrzeit)
twenty	zwanzig
to wait	warten

waiter	Kellner
to walk	gehen
wallet	Brieftasche, Geldbeutel
week	Woche
would (→ will)	würde

Unit 4 2-32

all around	ringsum, rundherum
arm	Arm
around	umher
to arrest	festnehmen
as	als
backup	Unterstützung, Verstärkung
bakery	Bäckerei
band	Band, Musikgruppe
blue	blau
bookshop	Buchhandlung
bread	Brot
brown	braun
to buy	kaufen
to call out	ausrufen, laut rufen
to catch	fangen
chair	Stuhl
clothes (*Pl.*)	Kleidung, Kleider
coat	Mantel
come on!	komm!, los!
to come over	herüberkommen
credit card	Kreditkarte
customer	Kunde, Kundin
dark	dunkel
dark blue	dunkelblau
doesn't (→ does not)	(er/sie/es) tut nicht
down	herunter, hinab
exit	Ausgang
face	Gesicht
far	weit (weg), fern
fast	schnell
flower	Blume
flower shop	Blumenladen
to follow	(ver)folgen
food	Lebensmittel, Essen
furniture (*nur Sg.*)	Möbel
furniture shop	Möbelgeschäft
German	Deutsch
to get away	entkommen
grey	grau
grocery	Lebensmittel-geschäft
handbag	Handtasche
Harrods	große britische Kaufhauskette
hat	Hut
hobby, hobbies (*Pl.*)	Hobby, Freizeit-beschäftigung
impossible	unmöglich
in front of	vor (örtlich)
to keep an eye on …	ein Auge haben auf …
to kiss	küssen
let's	lass(t) uns
light	hell
light green	hellgrün
like-minded	gleich gesinnt
lots of (*mit Pl.*), **a lot of**	viele, eine Menge

men's clothes shop	Männerbekleidungsgeschäft
might	könnte, möchte (möglicherweise)
mobile phone	Handy, Mobiltelefon
mother	Mutter
mysterious	unheimlich, mysteriös
new	neu
old	alt
on	auf, an
on Saturday	am Samstag
on the street	auf der Straße
orange	orange
perfect	perfekt, ideal
perhaps	vielleicht, eventuell
pink	rosa
to pull out	herausziehen
purple	lila
to push	stoßen
to push past	anrempeln
rain	Regen
right now	jetzt, in diesem Augenblick
to run	rennen
to run up	angelaufen kommen
scarf	Schal
shirt	Hemd
shoe	Schuh
shop assistant	Verkäufer(in)
shopping list	Einkaufsliste
silly	dumm, albern
size	(Kleider-)Größe
skirt	Rock
small	klein
to stay	bleiben
stole (→ to steal)	stahl, hat gestohlen
suspect	Verdächtige(r)
suspicious	verdächtig
table	Tisch
thank you	vielen Dank, danke
tie	Krawatte
tired	müde
towards	nach, zu, in Richtung
trousers (*nur Pl.*)	Hose
us	uns
warm	warm
to watch	beobachten, (an)schauen
white	weiß
wife	Ehefrau
winter	Winter
winter coat	Wintermantel
yellow	gelb
young	jung

Unit 5 2-33

also	auch, ebenfalls
always	(schon) immer, ständig
before	bevor
to book	buchen, reservieren
bought (→ to buy)	kaufte, hat gekauft
break	Pause
caught (→ to catch)	fing, hat gefangen
centre	Zentrum, Innenstadt
certainly	sicher, gern, gewiss
computer	Computer

different	unterschiedlich
don't have to (→ do not have to)	nicht müssen
double	doppelt, Doppel…
double room	Doppelzimmer
Edinburgh	Edinburg
to forget	vergessen
found (→ to find)	fand, hat gefunden
to go on holiday	in den Urlaub fahren
good afternoon	guten Tag
guidebook	Reiseführer, Ratgeber
had (→ to have)	hatte, hat gehabt
highland	Hochland
himself	er selbst, selber
holiday	Urlaub, Ferien
hotel	Hotel
how many	wie viele
information (*nur Sg.*)	Information(en)
Internet	Internet
to leave	hier: abfahren (Zug)
luckily	glücklicherweise
lucky	glücklich
midday	Mittag
much	viel, sehr
must	müssen
mustn't (→ must not)	nicht dürfen
needn't (→ need not)	nicht müssen
never	nie, niemals
night	Nacht
non-smoking	Nichtrauchen, Nichtraucher…
only	nur, bloß
to organize	organisieren
to pack	packen
page	Buchseite
paid (→ to pay)	zahlte, hat gezahlt
Past Tense	Vergangenheitsform (Grammatik)
to pay	(be)zahlen
phone number	Telefonnummer
platform	Bahnsteig
practical	praktisch, anwender-freundlich
Present Tense	Gegenwartsform (Grammatik)
to print	drucken
to put	setzen, stellen, legen
to put into	hier: eingeben (in den PC)
queue	(Menschen-) Schlange
receptionist	Empfangs-mitarbeiter(in)
to relax	entspannen, ausruhen
rental	Miete, Miet…
rental car	Mietwagen
replied (→ to reply)	entgegnete, hat entgegnet
return (ticket)	Fahrschein für Hin- und Rückfahrt
said (→ to say)	sagte, hat gesagt
Scotland	Schottland
seldom	selten
seller	Verkäufer(in)
single	einzeln, Einzel…
single (ticket)	Fahrschein für die Hinfahrt

single room	Einzelzimmer
to smoke	rauchen
smoking	Rauchen, Raucher…
stressed	gestresst
suitcase	Koffer
tent	Zelt
to thank	danken
thing	Ding, Sache
ticket	Karte, Eintrittskarte
ticket seller	Schalterbeamter am Bahnhof
tip	Tipp, Hinweis, Ratschlag
today	heute
told (→ to tell)	erzählte, hat erzählt
took (→ to take)	nahm, hat genommen
train	Zug
train station	Bahnhof
train ticket	Zugfahrkarte
to travel	reisen
travel agency	Reisebüro
upstairs	(die Treppe) hoch, nach oben, oberes Stockwerk
to use	nutzen, benutzen
was (→ to be)	war, ist gewesen
went (→ to go)	ging, ist gegangen
to wish	hoffen, wünschen
youth hostel	Jugendherberge

Unit 6 2-34

along	entlang
apple	Apfel
art	Kunst
art gallery, art galleries (*Pl.*)	Kunstgalerie, Gemäldegalerie (= Museum)
at night	nachts, in der Nacht
attacked	angegriffen
baby, babies (*Pl.*)	Baby, Säugling
bathroom	Badezimmer
bed	Bett
birthday	Geburtstag
body, bodies (*Pl.*)	Körper, Leiche
bodysnatcher	Leichenräuber
born	geboren
by car	mit dem Auto
called	genannt, mit Namen
case	(Kriminal-)Fall
castle	Schloss
Christmas	Weihnachten
church, churches (*Pl.*)	Kirche
city, cities (*Pl.*)	Stadt
crisps (*Pl.*)	Kartoffelchips
date	Datum
dead	tot
desk	Schreibtisch
diagonally opposite	schräg gegenüber
dinner	Abendessen
drove (→ to drive)	fuhr, ist gefahren
Easter	Ostern
end	Ende
Euston	Bahnhof und Stadtteil in London
evening	Abend
exciting	aufregend
excuse me	entschuldigen Sie/ entschuldige

fifth	fünfte/r/s, fünftens
film	(Kino-)Film
to find out	herausfinden
first	erste/r/s, erstens, zuerst
fourth	vierte/r/s, viertens
fridge	Kühlschrank
from … to	von … zu/bis
gallery, galleries (*Pl.*)	Galerie
gave (→ to give)	gab, hat gegeben
to get on	einsteigen
to get to	gelangen
ghost	Geist
got on (→ to get on)	stiegen ein, ist eingestiegen
graveyard	Friedhof
gym	Fitnessstudio
hungry	hungrig
inside	drinnen, innen
instant coffee	löslicher Kaffee
June	Juni
kettle	Wasserkessel, -kocher
knowledge (*nur Sg.*)	Wissen
language	Sprache
leaf, leaves (*Pl.*)	Blatt (Pflanze)
left	links
lights (*Pl.*)	Ampel
luggage	Gepäck
luggage rack	Gepäcknetz, -ablage
lunch	Mittagessen
lunch break	Mittagspause
magazine	Zeitschrift
main	Haupt…
main station	Hauptbahnhof
map	Stadtplan, Landkarte
May	Mai
medical	Medizin…
medical school	medizinische Hochschule
month	Monat
mystery	Geheimnis, Rätsel
national	national, inländisch
National Portrait Gallery	Staatliche Gemäldesammlung
news (*nur Pl.*)	Nachrichten, Neuigkeiten
New Year's Eve	Silvesterabend
nineteenth century	neunzehntes Jahrhundert
north	Norden, nördlich
opposite	gegenüber
past	an … vorbei
place	Ort
portrait	Porträt, Bildnis
to pour (out)	(ein)gießen, einschenken
rack	Ständer, Regal
rang (→ to ring)	läutete, hat geläutet
research	Forschung
reservation	Vorbestellung, Reservierung, Buchung
reserved	reserviert
restaurant	Restaurant, Speiselokal
right	rechts, richtig
to rob	rauben
robber	Räuber(in)
robbery, robberies (*Pl.*)	Raub

sandwich, sandwiches (*Pl.*)	belegtes Brot, Sandwich
school	Schule
Scott Monument	Denkmal für Sir Walter Scott
season	Jahreszeit, Saison
seat	Sitz, Platz
second	zweite/r/s, zweitens
to sleep	schlafen
Spain	Spanien
stairs (*Pl.*)	Treppe
still	noch (immer)
story, stories (*Pl.*)	Geschichte
straight	gerade, geradlinig
student	Student(in), Schüler(in)
summer	Sommer
teabag	Teebeutel
television	Fernsehgerät, Fernsehen
thermos	Thermoskanne
third	dritte/r/s, drittens
thought (→ to think)	dachte, hatte gedacht
through	durch
toilet	Toilette
tomorrow	morgen
tour	Tour, Rundgang
tourist	Tourist(in)
town	Stadt
trip	Reise, Fahrt
to turn	abbiegen
umbrella	Regenschirm
Valentine's Day	Valentinstag
view	Blick, Ausblick
watch, watches (*Pl.*)	(Armband-)Uhr
weekend	Wochenende
well	gut
year	Jahr

Unit 7 2-35

to ache	schmerzen, weh tun
ago	vor (zeitlich)
ambulance	Krankenwagen
any	irgendwelche
arm	Arm
at the doctor's	beim Arzt
to attack	angreifen
attacker	Angreifer(in)
bad	stark (bei Schmerzen)
bandage	Verband
to be on fire	in Flammen stehen, brennen
bottle	Flasche
to break	(zer)brechen
briefcase	Aktentasche
broken	gebrochen, zerbrochen
cat	Katze
to close	schließen
clue	Hinweis
cold	Erkältung
cold	kalt
colleague	Kollege, Kollegin
cough	Husten
crime scene	Tatort
curtain	Vorhang

to cut	abschneiden, durchtrennen, abschalten
dear	liebe/r/s
didn't (→ did not)	tat nicht, hat nicht getan
downstairs	unten, nach unten, unteres Stockwerk
drink	Schluck, Getränk
drip	Tropf
ear	Ohr
eye	Auge
finger	Finger
foot, feet (*Pl.*)	Fuß
for	lang (Zeitraum), für
Future	Zukunft (Grammatik)
ground	Boden
hand	Hand
to happen	passieren
head	Kopf
headache	Kopfschmerzen
heart	Herz
to hit	stoßen, schlagen
hospital	Krankenhaus
hot	heiß
hour	Stunde
I'll (→ I will)	ich werde
injured	verletzt
job	Arbeit
to keep	bleiben, halten, bewahren
key	Schlüssel
kiss	Kuss
knee	Knie
left (→ to leave)	hinterließ, hat hinterlassen, verließ, hat verlassen
leg	Bein
to lie	liegen
light	leicht
light	Licht
lying (→ to lie)	liegend
mouth	Mund
muscle	Muskel
muscleache	Muskelkater
neighbour	Nachbar(in)
next	nächste/r/s
nose	Nase
nurse	Krankenschwester
pain	Schmerz
painting	Bild, Gemälde
Past Continuous	Verlaufsform der Vergangenheit (Grammatik)
PC (Police Constable)	Polizeibeamter, -beamtin
plaster	Gips
rag	Lappen, (Stoff-)Fetzen
to remember	sich erinnern
ride	Fahrt
running	triefend, laufend (Nase)
sad	traurig
saw (→ to see)	sah, hat gesehen
scene of the crime	Tatort
to scream	schreien
sleep	Schlaf
slowly	langsam
to sneeze	niesen

someone	jemand
sore	wund
stomach	Magen
to switch on/off	an-/ausknipsen
to take	mitnehmen, nehmen
terrible	schrecklich
thirsty	durstig
threw (→ to throw)	warf, hat geworfen
thriller	Thriller
throat	Kehle
throbbing	pochend
to throw	werfen
toe	Zehe
tooth, teeth (*Pl.*)	Zahn
toothache	Zahnschmerzen
tried (→ to try)	versuchte, hat versucht
to try	versuchen
victim	Opfer
waiting room	Wartezimmer
wall	Mauer
water	Wasser

Unit 8 2-36

after	nach, nachdem
to analyse	analysieren, auswerten
armchair	Sessel
arson	Brandstiftung
available	verfügbar, erreichbar
basin	Waschbecken
because	weil
bedroom	Schlafzimmer
boring	langweilig
broke (→ to break)	(zer)brach, hat gebrochen/ist zerbrochen
to brush	bürsten
to brush the teeth	die Zähne putzen
to burn	brennen
came (→ to come)	kam, ist gekommen
car horn	Hupe
carpet	Teppich
to clean	putzen
colour	Farbe
company	Firma, Gesellschaft
connection	Verbindung
to cook	kochen
cooker	Herd
corridor	Flur
crazy	verrückt
to cry	weinen
doorknob	Türknauf
favourite	Lieblings…
feeling	Gefühl
fire	Feuer
fire engine	Feuerwehrwagen
fireman, firemen (*Pl.*)	Feuerwehrmann
fire service	Feuerwehr
flame	Flamme
flat	Wohnung
floor	Boden
forensic	gerichtsmedizinisch
forensic scientist	Gerichtsmediziner(in)
fork	Gabel
freezer	Tiefkühler
garden	Garten

heard (→ to hear)	hörte, hat gehört
High Wycombe	Ort westlich von London
hung up (→ to hang up)	legte auf, hat aufgelegt
to hurry	sich beeilen
to hurt	verletzen
hurt	verletzt
insurance company	Versicherungsgesellschaft
jealous	eifersüchtig
to jump	springen
knife	Messer
to knock	klopfen
to listen	zuhören, hören
loud	laut
louder	lauter
mailbox	Mailbox (Handy), Briefkasten
meat	Fleisch
message	(Text-)Nachricht
motive	Motiv
nearly	beinahe
noise	Krach
oven	Ofen
to pick up	abnehmen (Telefonhörer), aufheben
picture	Bild, Foto
plate	Teller
police car	Polizeiauto
to prove	beweisen
to put out	löschen
radio	Radio
ran (→ to run)	rannte, ist gerannt
real	echt, wirklich
report	Bericht
scientist	Wissenschaftler(in)
to sell	verkaufen
to share	teilen
shelf, shelves (*Pl.*)	Regal
shower	Dusche
signal	Zeichen
skill	Fähigkeit
sofa	Sofa
sold (→ to sell)	verkaufte, hat verkauft
sound	Geräusch
spare	frei, Gäste…
spare bedroom	Gästezimmer
spoon	Löffel
stood up (→ to stand up)	stand auf, ist aufgestanden
strangled	erwürgt, stranguliert
tax, taxes (*Pl.*)	Steuer
the Yard	Scotland Yard
wardrobe	Kleiderschrank, Garderobe
wasn't (→ was not)	war nicht, ist nicht gewesen
weren't (→ were not)	waren nicht, sind nicht gewesen

Unit 9 2-37

1930s	30er-Jahre
alert	Alarm
already	schon, bereits
anybody	(irgend-)jemand

anyone	(irgend-)jemand
ate (→ to eat)	aß, hat gegessen
beautiful	(wunder)schön
beef	Rindfleisch
been (→ to be)	gewesen
to be on the alert	auf der Hut sein
biscuit	Keks
blond	blond
building	Gebäude
calf	Kalb
camera	Kamera
car rental agency	Autovermietung
CCTV (Closed Circuit Television)	Überwachungs-kamera, Video-überwachung
cheese	Käse
chicken	Hühnchen
to commit	begehen, verüben
cow	Kuh
crime scene investigation officer	Mitarbeiter(in) der Spurensicherung
done (→ to do)	gemacht
eaten (→ to eat)	gegessen
fat	dick, fett
fish	Fisch
funny	seltsam, komisch
future	Zukunft
gone (→ to go)	gegangen
good-looking	gut aussehend
had (→ to have)	gehabt
has been kidnapped	wurde entführt
helpful	hilfreich, hilfsbereit
holiday flat	Ferienwohnung
immediately	sofort, auf der Stelle
incident	Ereignis, Zwischenfall
incident room	Einsatzzentrale
to interview	befragen, verhören
just	gerade, soeben
to kidnap	entführen, kidnappen
lamb	Lamm
lately	kürzlich
letter	Buchstabe
license plate number	Autokennzeichen
life	Leben
may	dürfte, könnte (möglicherweise)
Mercedes	Mercedes
to mix	mischen
modern	modern
moustache	Schnurrbart, Schnauzer
to move	bewegen, umziehen
movie	(Kino-)Film
officer	hier: Polizei-beamter, -beamtin
orange juice	Orangensaft
parked	geparkt
Past Participle	Partizip Perfekt, Partizip II (Grammatik)
peanut	Erdnuss
personal	persönlich
pig	Schwein
police station	Polizeirevier
pork	Schweinefleisch

potato, potatoes (*Pl.*)	Kartoffel
Present Perfect	Perfekt (Grammatik)
probably	wahrscheinlich, eventuell
question tag	Frageanhängsel (Grammatik)
rainy	verregnet, regnerisch
to rent	mieten
said (→ to say)	gesagt
scary	unheimlich
sea	Meer
seen (→ to see)	gesehen
to set off	abfahren, sich auf den Weg machen
to set up	aufstellen, einrichten
seventh	siebte/r/s
short	kurz
sixth	sechste/r/s
soap	Seife
spoke (→ to speak)	sprach, hat gesprochen
sunglasses (*nur Pl.*)	Sonnenbrille
to swim	schwimmen
tall	groß (gewachsen)
that's a pity	das ist schade
thin	schlank, dünn
tomato, tomatoes (*Pl.*)	Tomate
turkey	Truthahn
twice	zwei Mal
veal	Kalbfleisch
vegetable	Gemüse
wig	Perücke
witness, witnesses (*Pl.*)	Zeuge, Zeugin
won't (→ will not)	nicht werden
word	Wort
worried	besorgt
writer	Schriftsteller(in)
written (→ to write)	geschrieben
wrote (→ to write)	schrieb, hat geschrieben
yet	bisher, schon

Unit 10 2-38

a few	ein paar
as … as	so … wie
assault	Überfall, Angriff
badly	böse, stark
to be out of shape	nicht in Form sein, untrainiert sein
become	werden
best	beste/r/s, am besten
better	besser
bike tour	Fahrradtour
brought (→ to bring)	brachte, hat gebracht
to cheer	jubeln
to create	erschaffen, hervorbringen, machen
delicious	köstlich
to die	sterben
distance	Entfernung

dog	Hund
drug	Droge, Betäubungsmittel
dvd	DVD
early	früh
ever	jemals
failed	gescheitert, versagt, fehlgeschlagen
false	falsch, unecht
to feed	füttern
few	wenige
fit	gesund, (sportlich) fit
football	Fußball
to get married	heiraten
glad	froh
got (→ to get)	wurde, ist geworden
handcuffs (*nur Pl.*)	Handschellen
to have a shower	duschen
ice cream	Speiseeis
important	wichtig
jogging	Joggen, Laufen
kidnapping	Entführung
to kill	ermorden
lazy	faul
to lose	verlieren
mad	wahnsinnig
married	verheiratet
mastermind	Superhirn
met (→ to meet)	traf, hat getroffen
mile	Meile
Moriarty	Romanfigur von Sir Arthur Conan Doyle
nemesis	Erzfeind, Gegenspieler
Past Perfect	Plusquamperfekt (Grammatik)
polite	höflich
pre-recorded	vorher aufgezeichnet
pretty	hübsch
prison	Gefängnis
pub	Kneipe, Pub
quietly	leise
reception	Rezeption
shape	Form, Gestalt
slept (→ to sleep)	schlief, hat geschlafen
slow	langsam
smart	klug, gerissen
to smell	riechen
strawberry	Erdbeere
tennis	Tennis
terribly	schrecklich
than	als
tied up	gefesselt
to trick	überlisten
true	wahr, wirklich
to understand	verstehen
wardrobe door	Kleiderschranktür
weight	Gewicht
worse	schlimmer
worst	schlimmste/r/s, am schlimmsten